stop
look
breathe
create

An Hachette UK Company
www.hachette.co.uk

First published in the United Kingdom in 2017 by
ILEX, a division of Octopus Publishing Group Ltd
Octopus Publishing Group
Carmelite House
50 Victoria Embankment
London, EC4Y 0DZ
www.octopusbooks.co.uk
www.octopusbooksusa.com

Design, layout, and text copyright
© Octopus Publishing Group 2017

Distributed in the US by Hachette Book Group
1290 Avenue of the Americas
4th and 5th Floors
New York, NY 10104

Distributed in Canada by Canadian Manda Group
664 Annette St., Toronto, Ontario
Canada M6S 2C8

Publisher: Roly Allen
Editorial Director: Zara Larcombe
Managing Specialist Editor: Frank Gallaugher
Art Director: Julie Weir
Designer: Mina Bach
Assistant Production Manager: Lucy Carter

ISBN 978-1-78157-398-3

A CIP catalog record for this book is available
from the British Library

Printed and bound in China

10 9 8 7 6 5 4 3 2 1

stop
look
breathe
create

WENDY ANN GREENHALGH

ilex

Contents

EXPLORING THE WORLD MINDFULLY

When I was a child, I used to love wandering along the beach and picking up the brightly colored pebbles I found along the shoreline. I always wanted to take them home and would return with my small pockets bulging heavily. When I got my stones home—such a disappointment—no longer slippery with seawater, my beautiful pebbles had faded and I could hardly see the colors and patterns at all.

I was reminded of this the other day as I walked though a wet morning after a meditation session with some friends. The fallen leaves glowed yellow, orange, and green, their colors heightened by the rain. It is my practice—my *Stop Look Breath Create™* mindfulness practice—to notice these gifts cast in front of me so regularly by life. And it struck me then that mindfulness is very much like seawater or rainwater; when we are living mindfully, our mindfulness—that open, spacious state of awareness—holds everything we experience within it, soaking it like water. Through mindfulness, the brilliance, the beauty, the extraordinariness of things is revealed quite naturally to us.

When there is no "water," no mindfulness, when we're rushing and busy and caught up with the thoughts in our heads, the color and beauty can leach from life and we lose our sense of connection with them and with the joy and peace they bring. When this happens, we also lose the rush of energy and inspiration that comes from within and urges us to express ourselves creatively.

Stop Look Breathe Create is a simple creative mindfulness practice in four easy steps that I use to keep me connected to the rich waters of life and creativity. It has developed over more than twenty years of meditating, making art, writing, and creating, and I've shared it with countless people as a creative mindfulness teacher too. Like all good mindfulness practices, it's very simple and yet extremely profound. Practiced regularly over time, it has the potential to transform how we live, how we see, how we experience, and how we create. It can become, in other words, the clear water that reveals the beauty around us, and, indeed, the beauty within us, too.

WHAT IS MINDFULNESS?

Before I share the four Stop Look Breathe Create steps with you, it might be useful to ask the question, what is mindfulness? I often start my courses by asking this, and even if we know a lot about mindfulness it can be interesting to reflect and write a short definition. In class, we usually do this on Post-it notes and put them on the wall. People tend to come up with very similar answers to this question:

- Mindfulness is being present in the moment.

- When I'm mindful, I feel peaceful.

- Mindfulness is emptying the mind of thoughts.

- Mindfulness is being aware.

- Mindfulness is meditation.

- Mindfulness is watching the breath.

These are some of the common definitions and expectations of people who come to my classes. Perhaps yours are similar. The most simple and helpful definition of mindfulness I've found is this: mindfulness is a process of noticing what our experience is, whilst we're actually experiencing it. However even this description may leave us with unanswered questions about how we practice this 'process of noticing' and how it relates to creativity. So what follows is my definition of creative mindfulness. It won't quite fit on a sticky note, but it's as short and simple as possible.

MINDFUL DOING: In the "doing" part of mindfulness, we focus with kindly attention, on our breath, body, or sensory experiences. This gentle-hearted, active focusing helps us to become more mindful, moment-by-moment, of our thoughts, feelings, physical sensations in our body, and things in the world around us. When we're practicing creative mindfulness, this focus also includes an activity like drawing, writing, or taking photographs, which may enhance our focus. We gradually get better at focusing, becoming more absorbed and calm, and also more aware of the rush of thinking and reacting that habitually accompanies most of our experiencing.

For many of us, this calmer state of mind is a great relief, and may even be the reason we take up mindfulness practice.

However, it's important to remember that eliminating thinking or blocking out difficult emotions is not what mindfulness practice is for. The aim of mindfulness is to be aware of exactly what our experience is in the moment we're experiencing it, learning to self-compassionately make space for it. This may include noticing that we are thinking a lot, or an awareness of relaxation, joy, sadness or anxiety. When practicing creative mindfulness it means noticing the thoughts and feelings we have whilst we're creating too.

This intention to notice and gently hold our experience is much more powerful—and potentially much more liberating— than simply eradicating thinking and feeling, which is actually impossible to do since our brains are designed to think and our bodies and hearts made to feel. If we're aware of what we're thinking and feeling, we can begin to choose which thoughts we continue to think, or let go thinking, resting in the calm that comes as our mind quiets. We can do the same with our emotions, too.

That's the doing part of mindfulness: a practice of active and kindly focus and concentration that helps us become more aware of our thoughts, feelings, sensations, and experiences in the moment. These actions are the equivalent of turning on the faucet to let the water of mindfulness flow. As we practice, we may also notice in the small spaces between thoughts that start to appear, that we are beginning to experience a different way of being.

SIMPLY BEING: As our busy heads are calmed through a more sustained concentration, we begin to access a state of relaxed, open, mindful awareness that feels very different from our normal way of thinking and experiencing. Even more extraordinarily, this awareness seems able to observe that thinking and experiencing are happening without getting caught up in them!

Mindful awareness has been described in many different ways, but to give you some idea of what you're looking out for, let's say its presence can be noticed in a sense of spaciousness and openness; of stillness, inner quiet, and peace; or of alertness, absorption, and relaxation. It's sometimes also noticed as a feeling of gentleness, gladness, or emotional warmth that is very peaceful. This awareness seems to contain the entirety of our experience—our thoughts, emotions, and sensory experiences—yet at the same time isn't separate from them but closely, intimately connected to them.

When we're just resting in this awareness, simply being with each moment of our life without analyzing or thinking about it, we are effectively bathing in the water of mindfulness, resting in mindfulness as a state. In the "being" part of mindfulness we are in presence, open to the beauty of the world and our own creative inner nature. We're deeply

connected to the experience of
silky, sea-splashed pebbles on a
beach, or luminous rain-washed
leaves on the cement, to a feeling
of joy or a feeling of sorrow, to the
warmth of the sun or a cool breeze,
to the experience of drawing quietly,
the flow of writing a poem, the
stillness as we capture something of
beauty with our camera. In the being
part of mindfulness, all these things can
appear and pass away, floating by within the
water of mindfulness, there and then gone.

Being follows naturally from doing in
mindfulness practice. Mindfully doing leads to
being mindful. Turn on the faucet, and the water
will flow. When you do this, I'm sure you'll find,
as I have, that the beauty of the world and your own
natural creativity is suddenly much easier to
connect with.

Before I describe *Stop Look Breathe Create* in more detail, let's have a quick look at these four easy-to-remember steps:

1 . **STOP:** Press the pause button on life, slow down, and find some stillness.

2 . **LOOK:** See what's around you. Listen, smell, taste, and touch, too. It's all about noticing the beauty of the sensory world and the peace you can find in it.

3 . **BREATHE:** Connect with the tide of life, the breath as it moves in and out of your body.

4 . **CREATE:** After some time connecting with yourself and the world around you, express your experience with a doodle, a drawing, a photograph, some creative writing, or any creative expression that calls to you.

Now, let's break the practice down into its four parts so that you really know what you're doing. Then, we'll put it back together as you start the projects.

STOP

The *Stop* part of this practice is a reminder that we need to slow down and push the pause button on our lives. We rush around with our bodies tense and our minds whirring, ticking off things on our to-do lists—picking up the kids, finishing that report for work, going to the gym or the mall or that long-distance meeting—winding ourselves up into such a maelstrom of busyness that we lose touch with the small and nourishing pleasures in life, the beauty and peace of the world around us, and the deep satisfaction of being playful and creative. All acts of mindfulness, creative or otherwise, start with pausing and reminding ourselves that there is another way: the way of simply being.

MINDFUL STOPPING TIPS: Experiment with stopping at various times during your day and just doing nothing— a couple of minutes between emails every now and then, a couple more in the car before you hit the supermarket, and so on. You could also try stopping when you're walking somewhere and just stand for a minute. Slow down. Pause. See how that feels. Can you observe the spaciousness it provides amidst an otherwise busy day? Do you notice the whirr of thoughts and emotions more when they're not covered up by lots of rushing about? Try this for a week and write down anything you observe about your experience of stopping.

LOOK

Once we've stopped, the next thing we need to do is focus mindfully on one thing. We're entering the doing part of mindfulness here. Start with a sensory focus by looking, by noticing what's around you. What can you see? What is there in your environment that you haven't really paid attention to? Perhaps there's a tree outside the window, leaves shivering in the wind. Perhaps it's a painting on the office wall that you've never stopped long enough to really look at. Even the lines and whorls on our own fingertips are filled with minute and amazing detail that we can see once we pay attention.

The *Look* step is a reminder to come home to all your senses and really notice and be present to your direct experience of the world. As such, it's not just about looking but also about listening to the sounds around you, tuning in to the sensations in your body (hot or cold, tense or relaxed, etc.), smelling what there is to be smelled, even tasting with renewed attention to what you are tasting. That swig of coffee may never have tasted so good! When we tune in to our senses and our immediate experience of them, we instantly create an opportunity to move into that spacious feeling of simply being.

MINDFUL LOOKING TIPS: When you next *Stop* during your day, make a conscious effort to tune in to the world around you; *Look,* noticing what you see. What's there? Let your eyes rove around and come to rest on whatever seems to pull your attention. It might be anything—a stray leaf, a peeling poster on the wall, a bunch of flowers, the patterns of light and shadow on the ceiling. Notice what an incredibly rich visual world you live in, then try this with all your other senses too.

What can you hear, touch, taste, or smell? How does this sensory mindfulness alter how you relate to your world? What effect does it have on your body, mind, and emotions? This practice of tuning in through the senses is incredibly grounding and reassuring because it takes us out of our headspace and into the solidity of the sensory world around us. Try this for at least a week and write down anything you notice about your experience.

BREATHE

Once we've stopped and looked, then it's time to bring our attention to our breath and just *Breathe*. The breath is a great focal point because our body automatically breathes for us, which means our minds don't have to control it. I can remember sitting in meditation during a particularly stressful time of my life and feeling incredibly grateful that breathing was something I didn't have to figure out or fix. It felt like such a blessing to be able to hand this over to my body and sit as a silent witness to it. Whatever is going on in our lives, however busy we are, our breath is always there for us, flowing in and out like a wave, like the tide. Bringing our attention to the breath is a fast, simple way to ground ourselves in our direct experience of the present moment, to move into a more mindful state of being.

one-minute feather

MINDFUL BREATHING TIPS: Now that you've practiced stopping and looking, the next step is to add in mindful attention to the breath. Stay with this stage for a few minutes and follow these simple instructions:

- Pay attention to the breath as it moves in and out of your body and find the place in your torso where you can feel it best. This might be different from day to day—sometimes the lower belly, sometimes the solar plexus or the chest—so it's best to check in each time. That's part of the practice.
- Once you've located the place in your body where you most clearly feel the sensation of your breath, follow a breath all the way in as you inhale. Notice as you do so all the little movements of your body that happen as you take a breath; the chest and belly expand, ribs move to accommodate the air coming in, the diaphragm moves downward. *Breathe* naturally, not forcing it, and see what you notice as you breathe in.
- Then follow the out breath, noticing all the little sensations that occur as you exhale.
- See if you can follow a complete breath cycle, in and out, with total attention. If you find it hard to feel the sensations of the breath, try putting your hand on your chest, solar plexus, or belly.

- Continue this close attention to the breath, following your breathing all the way in and all the way out, all the way in and all the way out. Do this for at least five minutes.
- If you find yourself zoning out or thinking about other things, don't worry. This is what brains tend to do, so it's best to develop a sense of humor about it. Just be gentle with yourself and bring your attention back to the breath. Try to cultivate a kindly, self-compassionate attitude toward yourself and your wandering mind. Noticing you've gotten distracted then refocusing on the breath is a normal and important part of the practice, not an error.
- If your mind is especially restless, try giving your breath a little more attention. This doesn't mean trying to concentrate really hard; it's more an attitude of leaning into the breath, developing a greater curiosity about it. You can do this by not only following the breath all the way in and out, but also seeing if you can catch that moment when the tide of your breath turns, the moment when an in breath becomes an out breath and then an out breath becomes an in breath.

Now that you've tried this practice, how does it feel? What do you notice? If your mind is getting distracted regularly, don't worry. Just keep coming back to the focus on the breath. Importantly, please remember that the goal of mindfulness is not to stop ourselves from thinking; it's to be aware that we're thinking, aware that we're seeing, smelling, feeling, listening, aware of everything in our experience. That's when the magic happens. Try this for a week and write down what you notice about the experience.

ten-minute feather

CREATE

When we practice *Stop Look Breathe* we are changing our relationship to the moment, we are changing our relationship to ourselves, and we are also changing our relationship to the world around us. This just makes it all the easier to take things one step further and *Create*. This is the point where ordinary mindfulness becomes creative mindfulness.

Through practicing the sensitive, mindful opening of the first three steps we gain the opportunity to be creative in a completely new way. In simply being with ourselves as we are in the moment, in simply being with all the rich textures, colors, sensations, and sounds of the world around us, we allow our natural creative impulse to arise. When we do this, we can more easily express our innate creativity because, when we're practicing mindfulness, we are already immersed in a process of focus, absorption, and flow, which are the essential qualities of the creative process.

At this point, we can *Stop Look Breathe* and scribble a little drawing in our notebook, or *Stop Look Breathe* and take a photograph, or *Stop Look Breathe* and write a few words that express the moment. Creating follows naturally when we're more open to ourselves, our thoughts, and our feelings and we're connecting to the world around us. Through your own *Stop Look Breathe Create* practice, you can discover this for yourself.

Too early to be awake, Membranous sky of grey clouds, windy ocean of leaves, the chuckle of gulls, unquiet dreams.

HOW TO USE THIS BOOK:
A Little Creativity & Mindfulness Every Day

The more we practice mindfulness, the more we can move away from frantic doing and rest in that state of simply being. However, if we wanted to run a marathon, we wouldn't expect to suddenly put on our running shoes and jog twenty-six miles, we'd have to train. Similarly, if we want to live in that state of calm, open awareness, we can't expect to get up one morning and BE there, we need to train for this too.

If we've been neglecting the creative side of ourselves for a long time, because of hectic work schedules and busy family lives, then we also can't expect to suddenly become fully fledged Picassos overnight. We need to be gentle with ourselves and give it some time.

I've found the key to this is small enjoyable doses of mindfulness and creativity every day. So to get the best from this book and enjoy the benefits of creative mindfulness I suggest you make time for a little *Stop Look Breathe Create* most days. Once you've developed the habit it will become almost effortless. I found it incredibly easy once I started because I was having so much fun with it.

STOP LOOK BREATHE CREATE
Creative Mindfulness Tips

1. Add five to ten minutes of the *Breathe* practice to your day (see page 20). This can be done anywhere: commuting home on the train, waiting in your car on a school run, sitting in your favorite chair at home, and so on. While you are developing the mindfulness habit, it will work best to set a time for this and commit to it, as, inevitably, if we try and fit it in around all our other pressing daily tasks, it has a tendency to get sidelined. Make sure you turn off your mobile phone during mindfulness practice, too, so you don't get distracted.

2. Start by practicing *Stop Look Breathe* (starting on page 16) for a full week, including five to ten minutes of the *Breathe* practice each day, before moving on.

3. Once you have a week under your belt, allow yourself to savor the creative projects in this book. Each project has a brief introduction, photography, drawing, and writing activities. Then, at the end, you'll find an extra tip for practicing mindfulness that will take you a little deeper. The projects in this book are a complete creative mindfulness course and should be done in sequence from one to ten. How long you spend on a project is entirely up to you, but I'd suggest you take at least a week, doing the photography, drawing, or writing activities for a couple of days each. If you want to do them for longer, that's great; you could do a project a fortnight, or one a month. See what works for you, but little and often is better than lots on rare occasions!

4. Always remember to start your *Create* sessions with five minutes of *Stop Look Breathe* before you move on to enjoying the creative activities. How long should you take to do each *Create* activity? Really, the answer is: as long as you want! I find that once I've started drawing, writing, or taking photos, I lose my sense of time entirely. Occasionally, I've specified an amount of time for an activity, but if I don't, use ten minutes as your minimum. This is a realistic amount to fit into even a busy day, and you can always expand this if you've got the time or are really enjoying yourself (which I'm expecting you will).

5. If at any point you find my suggestions restrictive, please feel free to ignore them. If I say "try using charcoal" and you hate charcoal and every bone in your body is shouting "watercolor pencils," then go for it. This is all meant to be a pleasure. It's also meant to take you just slightly out of the "known zone." The ten-minute minimum time suggestion is here for that reason. Ten minutes usually takes us past our boredom threshold, past the point where we think we've got a total handle on things, and tips us into new territory where we let go and explore more. Over time, you may increase this lower limit, pushing up to fifteen, twenty, or even thirty minutes.

6. Finally, a word about art materials: Luckily, you don't need expensive art supplies or a professional camera to practice *Stop Look Breathe Create*. I'll make some suggestions about materials you might like to use at the beginning of each activity, but feel free to improvise with what you've already got at home. My kit is small and basic—my trusty 5.5×5.5-inch (14×14cm) sketchpad, my mobile phone, a couple of black pens, a graphite stick, and some water-soluble colored pencils—all easily transported in a small bag, or even my pocket. This means I can *Stop Look Breathe Create* anytime, anywhere.

PRACTICE—NOT PERFECT

Stopping, looking, breathing, creating—this mindful connection to things gives me so much joy, so much inspiration. When I practice these, no day is without some beauty, some peace, some happiness. I just have to be open to them, and *Stop Look Breathe Create* is the door.

However, it's important to remember that *Stop Look Breathe Create* is all about mindfully connecting to the world and enjoying the process of creating. It isn't about finishing objectively accurate drawings, creating an end product, getting a good grade, or developing perfect techniques. In other words, what we end up with isn't as important as the experience we had while doing it.

Since we have generally learned to compare, criticize, and strive for perfection in our creative efforts, this approach to creating is actually pretty radical. It encourages us to relax and enjoy the process, playing, exploring, and taking pleasure in creativity like we did as children rather than worrying about end results. So enjoy the mindful practice of *Stop Look Breathe Create* and don't worry about what you'll get out of it. The experience is the reward.

Wild Flower
Meadow
5min sketch

PROJECT 1

The ground beneath our feet

How often do you notice where you're walking and how it feels in your body to walk there? The still, grounded presence of the earth below us is often a forgotten element in our busy lives. We get so caught up in the whirl of living that we easily disconnect from our physical experience of it, including disconnecting from our bodies. This first project is all about starting to notice and experience the ground in more mindful and creative ways, coming home to ourselves and to our bodies as we do so.

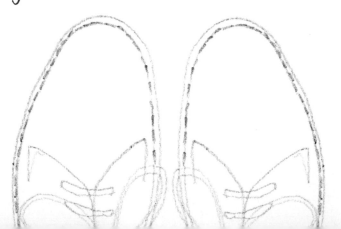

STOP—LOOK—BREATHE

- During this project, take time to mindfully feel your way into your body. How does it feel when you wake in the morning or when you're sitting between emails at your desk? How does your body feel when you're standing, waiting for the kettle to boil? *Stop Look Breathe* and notice the sensations of lying, sitting, standing, or any activity at all that you can pause to observe.

- Take a blanket and go lie down on the ground in your garden, in a local park, or out in the countryside. *Stop Look Breathe* and notice the sensations of the earth beneath you. How does it feel? How does your body feel lying there? Do you get some sense when your eyes are closed of the presence of the earth beneath you? What's that like?

- Now bring the same mindful attention to your body when it's walking. Walking is a very important part of the *Stop Look Breathe Create* practice.

- Walk slowly (slower than normal) and practice looking at the ground beneath your feet as you do so. Just watch it pass. Really notice the sensation as the soles of your feet make contact with the ground as you walk—heel, ball, toe, heel, ball, toe. Notice how your weight shifts from foot to foot. *Breathe* and notice your breath moving in and out of your body as you walk.

- Practice this mindful walking and careful attention to the sensations in the body for at least five minutes before you start creating, and practice it while you're creating, too.

FOUR TIPS FOR MINDFUL PHOTOGRAPHY

These are my four essential tips for mindful photography. Take some time to read and remember them so you can use them whenever you take a photograph.

1. **STOP** when you find something you want to photograph, but don't look at it through your camera screen just yet.

2. **LOOK** at this scene in a broad way first, allowing things of interest to jump out at you, then focusing on details after.

3. **BREATHE.** Feel the air move in an out of you, opening you to a sense of the space you're in and of the space between you and what you're looking at.

Repeat steps **1**, **2**, and **3**, varying your position; stand close, then farther away; stand to the side, above, or below what you're looking at. Now repeat *Stop Look Breathe* again, this time looking through the screen or viewfinder of your camera rather than with your eyes. Notice how this "artificial eye" changes things. Try *Stop Look Breathe* with the camera and then *Stop Look Breathe* with your eyes again. Keep switching between the two until you feel you've really seen what's in front of you clearly and new and surprising details begin to present themselves to you. And then ...

4. **CREATE!** Take the photo. You can repeat the whole four-step process until you've taken as many photos as you want.

CREATE:
PHOTOGRAPHY

You Will Need:

THE BASICS:
A camera or
mobile phone.

- After walking, *Stop and Look* closely at the ground beneath your feet where you're standing. *Breathe* and have a strong sense of the breath being grounded right down through the soles of your feet into the earth.

- What can you see? Take a photograph of the ground beneath your feet, this little patch of the world you're currently occupying. This photo may include your feet if you wish. Use the Four Tips for Mindful Photography, so that you really notice the ground you're standing on. Is there cracked cement or grass? Is it dusty or slick with rain? What patterns, textures, and colors do you see?

- Mindful photography is all about slowing things down and really being present, not rushing to click that button and move on. The longer you take, the more you'll enjoy it because you'll have been in the moment and fully aware. When you're ready, walk on and repeat the same *Stop Look Breathe Create* process, taking a photo somewhere else.

- Take many photographs in different places, noticing the ground *with your feet*, not just your eyes, as you do so. Grass feels very different to walk on, for example, than a gravel path. Focusing on sense impressions now will mean you remember this particular moment and place in a rich, sensory way when you look at your photos later.

*Patch of
dry grass* →

FOUR TIPS FOR MINDFUL DRAWING

Here are my four essential mindful-drawing tips. Take time to read and practice these, too.

1. Drawing is something we do with our whole body, not just our eyes and our hand. We need to connect and check in mindfully with our body when we draw. Notice what it feels like to hold the pen in your hand, the places it rests on your knuckles or the pads of your fingers. Notice the movement of your wrist, arm, and shoulder as you draw. Notice if you're holding any tension in your body and relax this on an out breath.

2. Check in with your breath regularly. It's very common for us to hold our breath when we're concentrating or if we've gotten caught

up in negative thoughts about the creative process. By checking in with our breath, we can learn to release tension before it builds, whether it's tension of the mind or the body.

3. As you practice drawing, try to be aware of your eyes leading your hand. As your eyes sweep over details, following a curve or a straight line, so your hand follows the eyes, making a curve and a straight line, too. The more you do this with awareness, the more naturally it will come.

4. Treat your drawing as a way of understanding, seeing, exploring, and getting closer to the world. Let go of notions that it has to look like a Da Vinci sketch!

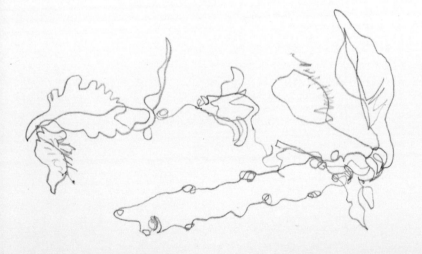

CREATE:
DRAWING

- Drawing is especially good for noticing things because it requires more time, focus, and concentration than simply taking a photograph. It is a form of intensely focused, mindful looking, and finely tuned looking skills are everything. I view my process as looking and then moving a pen around. Try that view on for yourself and see how it feels.

- Please remember, when we practice *Stop Look Breathe Create*, the aim isn't to produce "perfect" drawings but rather to draw in a way that helps us explore what we're seeing and relate to it more mindfully with a greater sense of connection and enjoyment.

- To help you move away from results-driven drawing in this project, I'd like you to draw without looking at the marks you're making on the page. Just *Look*, allowing your eyes to travel over things, moving up, down, and around them, and let your hand and drawing instrument follow your eyes. Try positioning your sketchbook to the side of you, rather than on your lap, so you're less able to peek at your drawing in progress.

- This approach is called "blind contour drawing," and it encourages us to make sketching a process of mindful seeing rather than accurate representation. It supports us in letting go of our inhibiting inner critic a little because we know from the outset that there's absolutely no chance we'll be able to do a "perfect" drawing this way!

- Don't feel you have to draw everything you see; that could be a little overwhelming. It might be that you get interested in one particular detail— the cracks in the earth for example, or the pattern of lines made by spears of grass on a lawn. If something engages your interest in this way, stay with it. Keep looking and continue drawing.

- When you've finished drawing in one place, move on, walking slowly and mindfully, until you find somewhere else of interest that you'd like to draw.

*Marks.
Made looking at the
grass NOT the page.*

FOUR TIPS FOR MINDFUL WRITING

These are my four essential mindful-writing tips. Keep these in mind as you do the *Create* writing projects and reread them occasionally if you need a reminder.

1. We're going to use "free writing" for all the creative projects. When we free write, we write in a stream of consciousness without planning ahead. We write without it needing to be anything in particular or needing it to take any particular form. When we free write, it's okay to wander off the subject and then wander back again. We allow the words to spill onto the page in ones, twos, sentences—however they come. We let one sentence run into another without worrying about grammar or punctuation, and it's okay if we repeat ourselves. That's often just us circling around interesting ideas or enjoyable words or phrases. When we're free writing, we're

HAND LETTERING helps me be mindful of how I make my LETTERs...

just enjoying the flow of language and ideas, fast or slow, whatever comes. It's also fine to have pauses when the mind is quietly gathering itself. We can use these for some more *Stop Look Breathe* moments. Write in paragraphs, notes, bullet points, fragments, or with no structure at all. Do whatever feels natural to you. If a structure or form comes, let it. If it doesn't, don't worry.

2. Keep your pen moving forward and *don't read back over what you've written until you've finished*. This will help stop your inner critic from getting involved. Always keep the creating part of writing away from the editing and drafting.

3. You can be as factual or poetic as you like. Just remember, you have all the language you need. You already use it everyday to express yourself, so putting words down on a page needn't be a struggle. Don't feel you have to reach for fancy words either; express yourself naturally in the way that feels right for you.

4. As with drawing, when we write, we write with our whole bodies not only our eyes and hands. Check in mindfully with your body and breath from time to time to remind yourself of this.

CREATE:
WRITING

You Will Need:

THE BASICS:
A sketchbook
or notepad and
a pen or pencil.

- *Stop Look Breathe* and then write about what you see on the ground beneath your feet, and what it feels like to stand so still, just breathing and looking. See it, feel it, write it. It's right there; you don't have to make anything up or use your imagination. You can just write about your experience in the moment.

- Build up a rhythm of writing a little, returning to *Stop Look Breathe*, writing a little more, returning to *Stop Look Breathe*, then writing again. By doing so, your writing will always be grounded in your direct experience and will be fed by it. Keep moving between writing and sitting quietly and doing *Stop Look Breathe* until the stream of words stops. Sit quietly for a little longer with a strong awareness of the ground beneath your feet and of being grounded in your body, and then move on to another place and do the same thing again.

- For those who worry about not having any interesting ideas or who feel they're not very imaginative, this way of writing can be very liberating as it's just about describing what's right here in the present moment. For those with big imaginations, mindful writing can help turn the most ordinary everyday things into inspiration for a poem or story later.

most, mulch for the ... king o
ees some leaves rec... his sa
errated edges of che... ut —
toothed. the gentl... obes
silvered by frost, wind... nest
asons. sweet chestn... musk
soft pelted, but roug... o the
bare toes, bare na... sunn
sandals gripping t... dust
wind, breezy toes! ... rly th
us, whorled like finge... ps.
have had five doze... gits
they snapped off — ... rid
moon crescents like t... inyp
finger nails curled i... a fist
just take it home, dr... go
and mind still feeling... pla

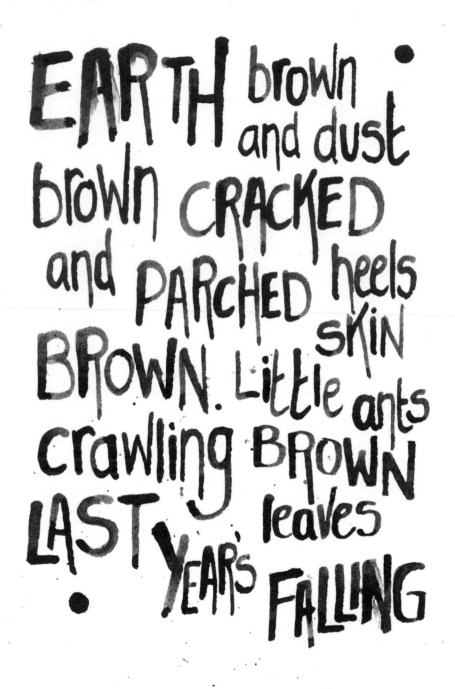

PROJECT 2

The sky above us

How often do you look up or notice anything
above eye level? In the busy, crowded cities we live
in and the crammed, full-speed lives we live, it can be
easy to disconnect with the spaciousness that's always
available to us if we only look up . Project 1 helped us
connect with our bodies and the Earth itself; this project
is all about connecting with the sky above us, slowly
attuning ourselves to the spaciousness up there and
finding experiences of it in our own body and mind
as we practice.

STOP—LOOK—BREATHE

- Continue with your mindful walking practice and try some mindful sitting too, feeling that chair beneath you as you *Stop Look Breathe*. Look up and notice what's there. Feel up too, if you can. What is your body's sense of the space above you if you close your eyes? Notice whether it feels the same or different from the ground beneath you. Remember to listen and smell, too, bringing in your senses one by one.

- Take time to *Stop* and *Look* at the sky, the scudding of clouds, the tops of trees, and the ridges of roofs, the flight of birds, and the crawl of airplanes. Feel the wind, the warmth of the sun beating down on you. Allow yourself to enjoy the wide-open spaces of the world above you.

- *Breathe* it all in, placing extra attention on the spaciousness of the in breath as your lungs expand and on the space above your head in the airy sky as you breathe out. See if you can connect with a sense of spaciousness inside you as well as outside you.

- Don't "over breathe." Just breathe normally and become aware as you do of the air leaving and entering your body, an endless tide. Try focusing your attention on your nostrils for a few moments, feeling the warmth of the out breath in them as you breathe out and the slightly cooler air as you breathe in, before returning to the spacious feeling of the in breaths in the torso.

CREATE:
PHOTOGRAPHY

You Will Need:

THE BASICS:
a camera or your
mobile phone and
a tripod (optional)

Continue using the Four Tips for Mindful Photography as listed on page 36. I'll assume you're always doing this from now on for each photography activity.

- Choose a patch of sky to befriend for a week, or longer. I suggest it's a patch of sky you can see and access regularly. It might be the sky through your bedroom window, the sky above your favorite tree, or the sliver of sky between two buildings that you can see from your desk at work.

- Choose a patch of sky and *Stop Look Breathe* with it at regular intervals during your week. Notice how it looks each time you observe it. In the morning it

might be a fine, light blue, with a scaling of feathery clouds. At noon it may be dark, heavily clouded, and looking like it's going to rain. In the evening it might be shading toward violet and punctuated by the flight of birds heading for their roost. At night, as you go to bed, is there a moon, stars, or only blackness?

- Check in with your patch of sky morning and evening, or choose to do it every hour on days where that is possible, but try to make these times regular and keep it up for at least a week. I stand at my bedroom window to do my mindful morning stretches and gaze up at the clouds, treetops, and birds. This is the natural time for me to *Stop Look Breathe Create* with the sky.

- Photograph your patch of sky standing in the same place every day, recording the space above you and the many changes it goes through over time. I particularly love the time element in this activity; it's like keeping a visual diary.

- You could try setting up a small tripod if you have one and leaving it in place so that your photos of the sky above you are always taken from exactly the same place and at the same angle each time.

- If you have a camera with manual settings, a tripod will also allow you to experiment with capturing movement in the sky using slow shutter speeds.

The automatic shutter speeds are quite fast and will freeze a bird in flight, but a longer exposure will record the blur of feathers as it passes. You'll just need to make sure your photo isn't too dark or too bright by adjusting the aperture (ƒ/stop). If you haven't done this before, there are lots of tutorials online. It's quite easy to work out and fun to experiment with.

- If you get more technical with your camera, make sure you always use the Four Tips for Mindful Photography before you take your photograph!

CREATE:
DRAWING

You Will Need:

THE BASICS:
A sketchpad or
notebook and
a pencil or pen.

EXTRAS:
Colored pens,
pencils, or chalks.
(Water-soluble
pencils are
fun to use!)

Continue using the Four Tips for Mindful Drawing
on page 40. I'll assume you're doing this from now on
as we explore other drawing activities throughout this book.

- Take yourself out for a mindful walk and see what catches your eye up
  above you. You don't need to know why you're drawn to something; just
  allow yourself be open to what's present. It might be a line of trees on
  the horizon, a crane over a building site, or even the roof and chimney
  of your own house.

- Once again, I'd like you to draw without looking at the page. There will be
  lots of time for looking at your paper later, I promise, but right now we're
  focusing on letting go and enjoying our drawing.

- *Stop Look Breathe* and allow your eyes to trace over what you're looking
  at, then put your pencil to the page and let your hand make the same
  movement your eyes are making. Eyes up along a chimney pot, pencil up
  along a chimney pot; eyes following the curve of an edge, pencil following
  the curve of an edge. Relax and *Breathe* into this reciprocal movement.

- I'd also like you to keep your drawing instrument on the paper while you do this, so that you make a continuous line. If you need to go back over a detail, do so by retracing a line, rather than lifting up from the page. These continuous line drawings are another way of having fun with drawing and treating it lightly as a way of seeing and engaging more mindfully, rather than trying to make perfect reproductions.

- When you've finished drawing, and before you take a look at the page, close your eyes briefly. When you finally open your eyes and look at your drawing, notice what thoughts or feelings emerge. Do you feel happy, disappointed, or surprised by what you see? Be mindful of your response to what you've left on the paper.

- Try drawing several things using the continuous line and blind contour drawing combination and then, if you wish, you can start looking at the page and lifting your pen from the paper.

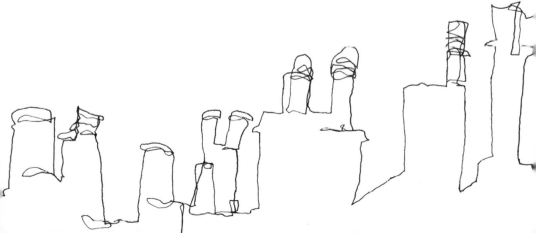

Pen following
movement of
branches. Not
looking at the page.
Reorienting my pen
for each new trunk.

Windy Trees

CREATE:
WRITING

You Will Need:

THE BASICS:
A sketchbook
or notepad and
a pen or pencil.

Use the free writing technique described in the Four Tips for Mindful Writing on page 44; do so for each writing project throughout the rest of this book, unless I say otherwise.

- Writing is a wonderful creative medium because we can bring in all the senses—something that photography or drawing can't. Once you've described what you see when you *Look* up in the world above you, then write about the sounds, sensations, and smells that are part of your experience to create a piece of writing full of all your sensory impressions.

- Focus on each sense in turn and remember to move between sensing and writing, sensing and writing. Sensory writing is always incredibly appealing to read, and by focusing on all the senses, your descriptions will become even more vivid and your mindfulness much more complete.

- You may also want to write about your feelings in response to the subject of your writing. Perhaps the freewheeling flight of a flock of pigeons overhead makes you feel energized and happy, or the bare branches of the winter trees seem desolate and cold. We can even attribute our emotions to the things we're looking at through the use of personification. We might write that the flock is joyous, or the trees are lonesome, for example, as if they too had human feelings. We just have to remember to *Stop Look Breathe* and notice what we're feeling so that we can *Create* and write about it.

feather, laid on like cream, wispy trailers
white combed all one way, milk smoo
the centre, so thick and curdy I'd
ir my finger in them, bring it out heavy
no sticky - lick off, lick clean - if I could
oth on your lip, on your chin when you
ere a child, long glass, ice cold from the
idge, everyone wearing a ring of milk, curving
no the sky today a cloud horizon the
eeds distance to appreciate it, the
urve of the earth for this striated
ilky sky. Air feels thick and warm t
eat building below the growing cloud
ver, the floodlights from the stadi
dull grey wavering stalks stirring th
kyline, reeds in the horizon line. A
dedly moving, just wavering too, laid
p, banked in layers of heat, waiting
e later rain. I think. Tree tops barel
oving up there, but here my page
ffling in a scurrying ground breeze

PRACTICING MINDFULNESS:
Feeling Spacious

Remembering to *Stop Look Breathe* and allow ourselves to experience a sense of spaciousness amid the busyness of our lives can be one of the kindest and most loving things we can do for ourselves. It's part of my daily self-compassion practice, and I suggest you make it part of yours too. Self-compassion is an incredibly important part of mindfulness, and it's absolutely essential when we're being creative since we all have a tendency to be harsh with and overly critical of our creative efforts. We'll look at these self-critical tendencies more in Projects 3 and 7 in particular, but for now I'd like to invite you to explore how offering yourself the gift of "feeling spacious" can create a greater sense of gentleness, kindness, and warmth toward yourself and your creative process.

Shift e surge.
the hurry of wind
below twlet grass
bright green

- Make time at the beginning and end of your day to *Stop Look Breathe* and focus actively on the feeling of utter spaciousness on your in breath. Do this for a few minutes, allowing yourself to really rest in that feeling with each inhalation. Intentionally give yourself this awareness of spaciousness as a gift, as a reward for the day, or as a consolation for any troubles.

- You could do this at other times in your day too if you feel you need it, perhaps at any high-stress moments or when you're feeling particularly rushed.

- Our creativity needs and craves this kind and mindful spaciousness. We can be so rigid and unrelenting with ourselves when we create, so anxious to be perfect and not to make mistakes, so down on ourselves when we do make what we perceive as an error. Mindfully connect with the spaciousness of the in breath and the feeling of the space around you for a few moments before you *Create*, and hold the intention—almost as an affirmation—that your process of creating is a space where you're going to be as gentle and accepting of yourself as you possibly can be.

- If, in the middle of drawing, taking a photo, or writing, you notice you're getting cramped and tense or critical about things, then *Stop* for a few moments, reconnect with that kindly intention, and deliberately *Breathe* that spacious in breath before you continue. By stopping at this time and focusing on the gift of spaciousness and breath in the body, we interrupt the start of what could be a long chain of negative thoughts and feelings. Over time, we retrain our brains toward more positive thought patterns.

The world in full color

What is your relationship to color?
Do some colors make your heart sing
while others bring you down?
What effect do your favorite colors have
on your mood, emotions, and even your body?
A mindful awareness of color can brighten
the grayest of dull, rainy days.
This chapter is all about exploring color creatively
and mindfully, and about learning to let go
and make space for our playful,
colorful, creative nature.

STOP - LOOK - BREATHE

At different times in our lives—and even at different times throughout our day—certain colors speak to us. When I was an art student, I used to dye my hair bright scarlet in the winter months because somehow it helped me beat the winter blues! Here's a simple way to feel within for the colors that are resonating with you today.

- *Stop Look Breathe* until your mind is calmer and you feel connected to your body. Then, bring your attention to the space in the middle of your chest. We can call this the "feeling space" because it's where we feel a lot of our emotions. There's another feeling space at our solar plexus too. See if you can get a sense of these places within you. *Stop Look Breathe* with them and then intuitively choose one to focus on.

- Place the question, "What color is here?" or simply, "What color?" into your feeling space and see what color comes to mind. You may see an image or hear or see a word in this mindful, somatic space. Go with this color, whatever it is, even if it's not your favorite or it seems to be a mixed up version of several colors.

- If no color emerges, then try going through the rainbow and placing each color, one by one, into the feeling space and seeing how that feels. Do this until you get a sense of the right color just for now, or just pick one, and work with that.

CREATE:
PHOTOGRAPHY

You Will Need:

THE BASICS:
A camera or
mobile phone.

- Go for a mindful walk and as you *Stop Look Breathe*, look out for your feeling-space color. If yours was a combination of colors, choose the main shade. If you saw a very specific shade—a pale, primrose yellow, for example—widen your search to include all shades of yellow, such as a yellow no-parking line on the road, a fallen leaf, a yellow scribble of graffiti on a wall, a pale yellow t-shirt displayed in a shop window.

- Whenever you see your color, *Stop Look Breathe* and stay with it, keeping in touch with your feeling space as you do. Notice how your mind, emotions, and body respond.

- Photograph anything and everything you find in your feeling-space color. As you do, the differences in these colored objects will start to become apparent and you'll see how the shiny yellow of a ceramic coffee mug reflects the light while the old paint on a door reveals texture more than reflection.

- Photograph in your normal mindful way and create a series of images all containing your feeling-space color.

- You could try this on different days, checking in each morning for your feeling-space color and then exploring the world looking for it.

CREATE:
DRAWING

You Will Need:

THE BASICS:
A sketchpad or notebook and water-soluble pencils or crayons.

EXTRAS:
Paintbrush and drawing inks.

- Find a few objects in your chosen feeling-space color. Choose things with strong, distinctive shapes to sketch; a blue flower is probably going to be more rewarding to draw than a blue bottle top, although mindfully drawing both will reveal new and interesting details.

- Use whichever approaches to drawing you are finding most useful and enjoyable (i.e., not looking at the page, continuous line drawing, or drawing normally).

- Select several water-soluble color pencils in your chosen shade. It's best to have a range from light to dark, for example pastel blue, cerulean, navy, and some turquoise thrown in for good measure.

- Begin with *Stop Look Breathe*, connecting with your feeling space and how the color makes you feel. As you draw, spend as much—if not more time—looking at your object as you do at your sketch.

- Experiment and play! Water-soluble pencils and crayons have an unpredictability to them that I particularly like, so they're good for learning to let go and embrace the creative opportunities of "accidents." Try shading, scribbling, dotting, dashing, and cross-hatching. Have fun mark making and experimenting, and discover a range of marks you can use to build up color and areas of shadow in your drawings.

- Now try adding water. Use water on the end of your finger or on a paintbrush to smudge your sketch, creating areas of tone or softening marks. You can also try dipping your pencil in water, or even leaving it in water for a while to soften the tip, and then drawing this way; it can create beautiful lines.

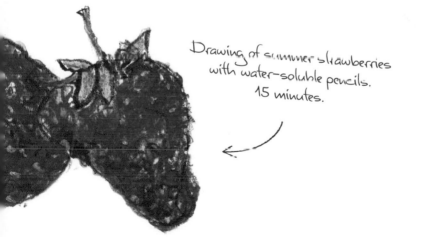

Drawing of summer strawberries with water-soluble pencils. 15 minutes.

CREATE: WRITING

You Will Need:

THE BASICS: A sketchbook or notepad and a pen or colored pencils.

- First, *Stop Look Breathe*, noticing your chosen color and the sensations and emotions in your feeling space. Notice what feelings were there to begin with and how the color affects these, if it does at all. Begin to free write, moving between periods of mindfully sensing your physical sensations and emotions in the feeling space and periods of writing or journaling what you discover. Memories associated with this color, free associations, or wild leaps of imagination, as well as current life situations, may emerge as you write. Let them appear as the color first appeared, unbidden and without censoring. See how much you can let go into the process. Continue with this until you feel you've written all you want to, or can. Try this with different colors on different days.

- Alternatively, start describing the colors of the objects you've been drawing or photographing using a series of similes. (Similes compare one thing to another using the words "like" or "as.") These similes don't have to make sense; just allow your imagination to supply you with some (however crazy) and write them down. Keep going until you run out of ideas. Then, come back to your color after a few moments of mindful walking, look at it again, breathing and relaxing, and see if any more ideas come. I find that the more I let go and write any old thing—foolishness, trash, nonsense—the more great stuff I come up with. Don't try to be poetic or make sense; just see what emerges. You can do this with more than one color and see which inspires the most extraordinary similes.

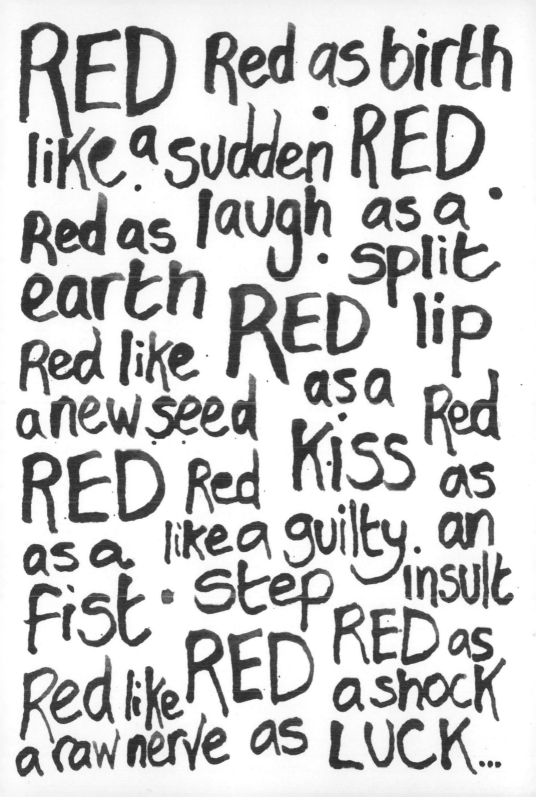

RED Red as birth
like a sudden RED
Red as laugh as a · split
earth RED lip
Red like as a
a new seed Red
RED Red kiss as
as a like a guilty · an
fist · step insult
Red like RED RED as
a raw nerve as a shock
LUCK...

PRACTICING MINDFULNESS:
Learning to Let Go

One of the biggest challenges we face is learning to let go and create uninhibitedly. Learning to let go and release control a little is important because when we hold on too tightly, we don't give ourselves and our creativity space to grow. Letting go relaxes, opens, and enlivens, giving our creativity space to thrive. Letting go can be scary though, and we hold on for lots of reasons. Here are some of the most common ones. Can you see how these can be combined into endless combinations of holding on, hesitating, and controlling?

- Self-criticism, inner judging, and comparing ourselves to others are types of holding on that say, "This mark, these words, they're not good enough. Even as I'm writing or drawing I'm going to censor myself, second-guess myself, put myself down. Look, that woman's drawing is much better than mine."

- Doubt and fear are types of holding on that say: "It's not good enough, I'm useless, I'm going to fail. What made me think I could do this? I'd better not start because it's all going to go horribly wrong."

- Perfectionism and expectations about how our creative efforts are going to turn out also make us try and control outcomes. "It's got to be as good as the one I did last week. It will be as good as the one I did last week. Oh no, I don't think it's going to be as good as the one I did last week!"

All of these are the mind resisting the natural, expressive flow of our inner creativity, but we can move beyond these holding-on habits with a little mindfulness. Here's how to practice mindfully letting go.

- Firstly, there's no point in telling ourselves to let go. I tried that for years, and it didn't work. Instead, shift your attention from all that thinking and trying and simply relax into the body, reconnecting with that self-compassionate spaciousness we explored in the previous project.

- Use *Stop Look Breathe* to find and relax any tension in the body. This physical releasing helps us to let go with our minds too.

- Intentionally choose an attitude of play and experimentation. Embrace creative chaos! You could even start a drawing, photography session, or piece of writing with the deliberate intention of scribbling, using weird lopsided angles, making your photos blurry, or writing like a five-year-old, with made-up words and no grammar. Go on, please, make a mess! Whenever I give this instruction in classes, the atmosphere in the room changes dramatically, everyone lightens up, their bodies relax and they seem to enjoy themselves so much more.

- For some people (myself included), the holding-on habit can be a strong one, so don't berate yourself if that's true for you. Mindfully notice how much you can embrace letting go, and how much you resist it. *Stop Look Breathe* with this resistance, then relax, and let go into the body some more.

- Please don't assume that experienced or professional writers, artists, and photographers don't have issues with self-criticism or holding on; they're just experienced and professional at it! They've been learning to work creatively with these issues for years.

- Let go in increments. As you make a mess and make glorious "mistakes," notice what giving yourself license to "just do it" feels like. Let the creative process direct you. I'm willing to bet quite a large amount of money that this feels much more colorful, free, and enjoyable.

Notice how many different colors I used to draw this "red" pomegranate. As soon as we Stop Look Breathe we start to see how there's no such thing as plain "red," or "yellow," "green," or "blue" either. In fact we're surrounded by so many varied and often subtle hues there aren't enough pencils to draw them.

Life's patterns & textures

The natural world and the cities we build all have their unique patterns and textures, and so do our moods and emotions, bodies and minds. From the spiral we find in seashells and ferns, to the grain of wood, to the repetition of windows in a row or rails in a fence, as we practice Stop Look Breathe, we start to become more mindful of the beauty and intricacy of the repeating patterns and textures that surround us. We also gain a greater awareness of the repeating patterns of our thoughts and feelings.

STOP—LOOK—BREATHE

- We can explore the patterns and textures of the world around us by choosing a specific pattern or texture before we go for a mindful walk. For example, you might choose a shape such as circles, a pattern such as stripes, or a texture such as spikey, then use *Stop Look Breathe* to discover these patterns, shapes, or textures in the world around you. You might see dark, wet stripes made by rain running down the dry bark of a tree, then you notice the same pattern again on an awning over a shop, and again in the lines painted on the road to slow traffic.

- Alternatively, you can go out for a *Stop Look Breathe* walk and just open (in the way we've been practicing) to the world around you. *Look* mindfully to see what attracts you on this particular day. One morning, for instance, I found myself struck by the pattern of branches on the trees in the park—that spreading-outward pattern, with the limbs of the tree always dividing and dividing again. This is a familiar natural pattern; we find it in plants and river deltas, and cracks in walls.

Charcoal rubbing
of tree bark

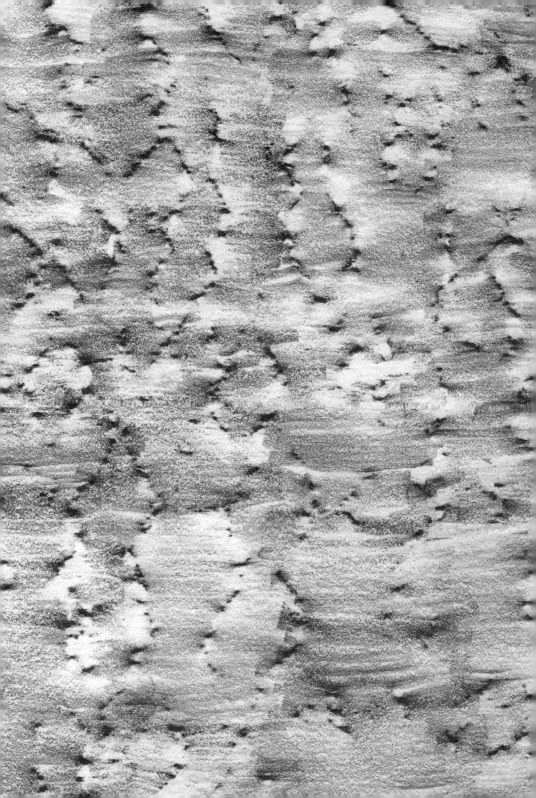

- Once a pattern like this has caught your attention, you can then direct the rest of your walk to staying mindfully attuned to seeing it, looking out for other similar patterns. When you do find it (and you will), you can then spend time with it, focusing on *Stop Look Breathe*. Once you become mindfully aware of these patterns and textures in the world, you will (just as you did with color) start seeing them everywhere.

- Try both of these approaches and see which you prefer. At first, you might find the second a little harder, but as time goes by and you become more sensitive and attuned to exploring the world this way, these natural patterns, shapes, and textures will start to become more and more accessible to you.

CREATE:
PHOTOGRAPHY

You Will Need:

THE BASICS:
A camera or
mobile phone.
EXTRAS:
Scissors, a glue
stick, and paper for
making montages
with your images.
after capture.

- With its capacity for taking fast, easy, and multiple images, as well as mass reproductions, photography is a great way to explore motifs of visual repetition and pattern. Using the guidelines in the *Stop Look Breathe* section of this project, record the repeating visual patterns you find. Let yourself become a little obsessive about it. (I've just spent a month photographing circles.) You could choose one or even two or three such patterns—spirals, rectangles, and parallel lines, for example—and spend a week photographing each of these when you find them. Just take your camera along wherever you go.

- Try printing these images out and curating them together into groups, grids, or long friezes. Create mini montages or collages that show this pattern.

- You'll start to see how the patterns are emerging not just in the world but in how you take your photographs too. For example, you may start to notice that when you photograph your parallel lines from a certain angle you get an interesting perspective. Here it is in one, two, three of your photos from the week and you really like this. You might not have been aware of this pattern when you were taking the photographs, but here it is! If you find a repeating pattern within your work, next time you go out for a *Stop Look Breathe Create* walk, use that pattern to take all your shots. Print them out again, and see what you think.

- Sometimes it's a theme or particular object that repeats itself and provides the pattern in our photography. For example, last year I suddenly noticed the self-seeded plants growing in the city streets where I live and took dozens and dozens of photos of them, all with the same camera angle and always in a square format. For you, it might be water coolers, sunsets, tulips, or people's feet—anything!

Once I started looking I found circles EVERYWHERE

CREATE: DRAWING

You Will Need:

THE BASICS:
A sketchpad and
the drawing media
of your choice
(i.e., pencil, charcoal,
pastel, crayon).

- Drawing is a wonderful medium for exploring texture
  and helping us to become more mindful not just of our
  dominant visual sense, but also of our felt sense, of the
  tactile relationship we have with the world.

- Pay attention to the visual textures around you. It might be
  the rough surface of bricks that draws you in, or the shiny
  smoothness of glossy leaves on a laurel bush.

- What is pleasant to the eye is often pleasant to the touch too.
  Close your eyes and touch this surface that persuaded you
  to *Stop Look Breathe* with it. What does it feel like? Explore it
  with your fingers. *Stop Touch Breathe.* If you feel self-conscious
  or vulnerable doing this in a public place, then practice
  somewhere you feel safe, such as your garden, or simply
  collect things you can take home and explore there.

- After some time touching, and with your eyes still closed, try
  drawing what you can feel. You can continue to feel the texture
  and shape with your non-dominant hand while you draw.

- Follow patterns, lines, or whorls with your fingers and draw
  them. If your fingers can feel ridges, draw them. When you do
  this, your mind will probably try and visualize what you can

Feeling tree bark
in the park
with my eyes closed.

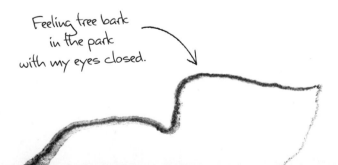

feel, it may even produce a little image of it. See if you can notice this happening. It's okay to draw from these mental images, but better still, let go of them and just intuitively make marks that seem to fit what your fingers are sensing without analyzing them too much. This is the difference between experiencing the world through the mind and experiencing the world directly through the senses.

- When you've done this with one texture, open your eyes and look at it again. How has your relationship to it changed? Do you feel you know it better, or in a different way?

- You could also take a rubbing of this texture by laying a sheet of paper over it and using a soft pencil, crayon, pastel, or charcoal to rub over the surface so that the textures are translated onto the page.

- Try building up a little collection of found textures over the course of a week or so, recording them in different ways. Start to notice your patterns. Which visual and tactile textures are you most drawn to? Which do you most enjoy relating to?

Stick drawn
with eyes shut
feeling with fingers
continuous line
texture of bark and
lichen dry and dusty

CREATE: WRITING

You Will Need:

THE BASICS:
A sketchbook or notepad and something to write with.

EXTRAS:
Large sheets of paper and colored pens or pencils.

- Throughout your day, stay mindful and aware of your senses. Or, choose to remain extra mindful at a particular time of day, such as when you walk home from work or are sitting having a well-earned coffee before you go and pick the kids up from school. Do this every day for a whole week, or longer if you wish.

- During this time, pay attention not just to what you see, but also to what you hear, smell, taste, and touch, practicing *Stop Look Breathe* with all your senses and free writing using the repetitive phrases: "Today I saw … Today I touched … Today I smelled … Today I tasted … Today I heard." Keep on repeating these phrases, building up a pattern and rhythm with the words.

Today I've heard
leaf lullaby
the shift & surge
of wind

Today I've felt
hot sun
and the slice
of shade

- Although you are still free writing, just letting what comes come, see if you can make space for longer, fuller descriptions to emerge. Instead of simply writing, "Today I heard … a blackbird," or, "Today I saw … a snail," see if, by really looking, listening, sensing, and paying close attention you find a more intimate and precise description. This doesn't mean you have to use elevated, poetical language; you can keep it simple, but real. Here's one of my recent ones: "Today I saw … a snail with a frill of moisture around it like a skirt."

- At the end of the week, write up your rhythmic diary of the senses onto a very large piece of paper using your colored pens or pencils. Choose a different color for each sense. Enjoy the patterns of colors as well as the rhythm of the words, and see what the sensory pattern and texture of each day or part of your day was like. Maybe you'll notice that certain things repeatedly get your attention, such as trees, water, or light. You might discover that you're more of a kinesthetic, touching, feeling person than you realized, or that you must really love the smell of that honeysuckle outside your window because you wrote about it every day.

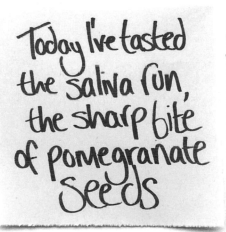

PRACTICING MINDFULNESS:
Discovering Our Creative Patterns

What have you learned about your habits, thoughts, feelings, and patterns around creativity in these first four projects? Take some time to reflect on the following:

- What part of this practice has given you the most consistent pleasure? Why?

- What do you find the most challenging? Why?

- What habitual patterns of thinking, feeling, or behaving have you discovered around creating now that you're being more mindful (i.e., procrastination, negative self-talk, disappointment, too little self-compassion, enthusiasm, concentration, feeling peaceful, a sense of pride)? Has how you relate to these patterns changed at all while practicing *Stop Look Breathe Create*? If yes, in what way?

- What new patterns have you established, and, if they feel good, how can you maintain them?

Hold each new answer or piece of information in your mind, noticing how it feels in your body. *Stop Look Breathe* with it for a while before you ask yourself more questions. Please practice lots of self-compassion during this exercise. It's not about making a list of how you've failed or what you've done wrong, but about kindly noticing any patterns that might be holding you back, or celebrating any natural tendencies or new habits that have been making you feel good.

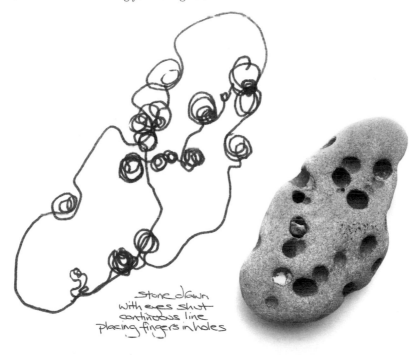

Stone drawn
with eyes shut
continuous line
placing fingers in holes

PROJECT 5

Water of life

From ice to rain, from swimming pools to puddles,
and from faucets to oceans, in this project we'll
be exploring water in all its many forms and
mindfully noticing its capacity for transformation.
Water has long been a metaphor for our emotions,
so in these activities we'll also be developing
a more fluid attitude to our feelings, bringing
more awareness to the shifting tides of our moods
and emotional life, and increasing our capacity
to just watch the flow with mindfulness.

STOP—LOOK—BREATHE

- Make water the focus of your mindful attention. Become mindful of how you respond to water through all of your senses, whether it's a cool drizzle on your face or the shower you take in the morning. How present and open can you be to this essential element?

- Make time to visit a larger and wilder body of water, perhaps taking a drive or hike to a local river, reservoir, lake, or even the ocean.

- *Stop Look Breathe* with water in all its forms, and as you do so take time to really experience how extremely different each of these forms is and how extraordinary this is (it's something we often take for granted).

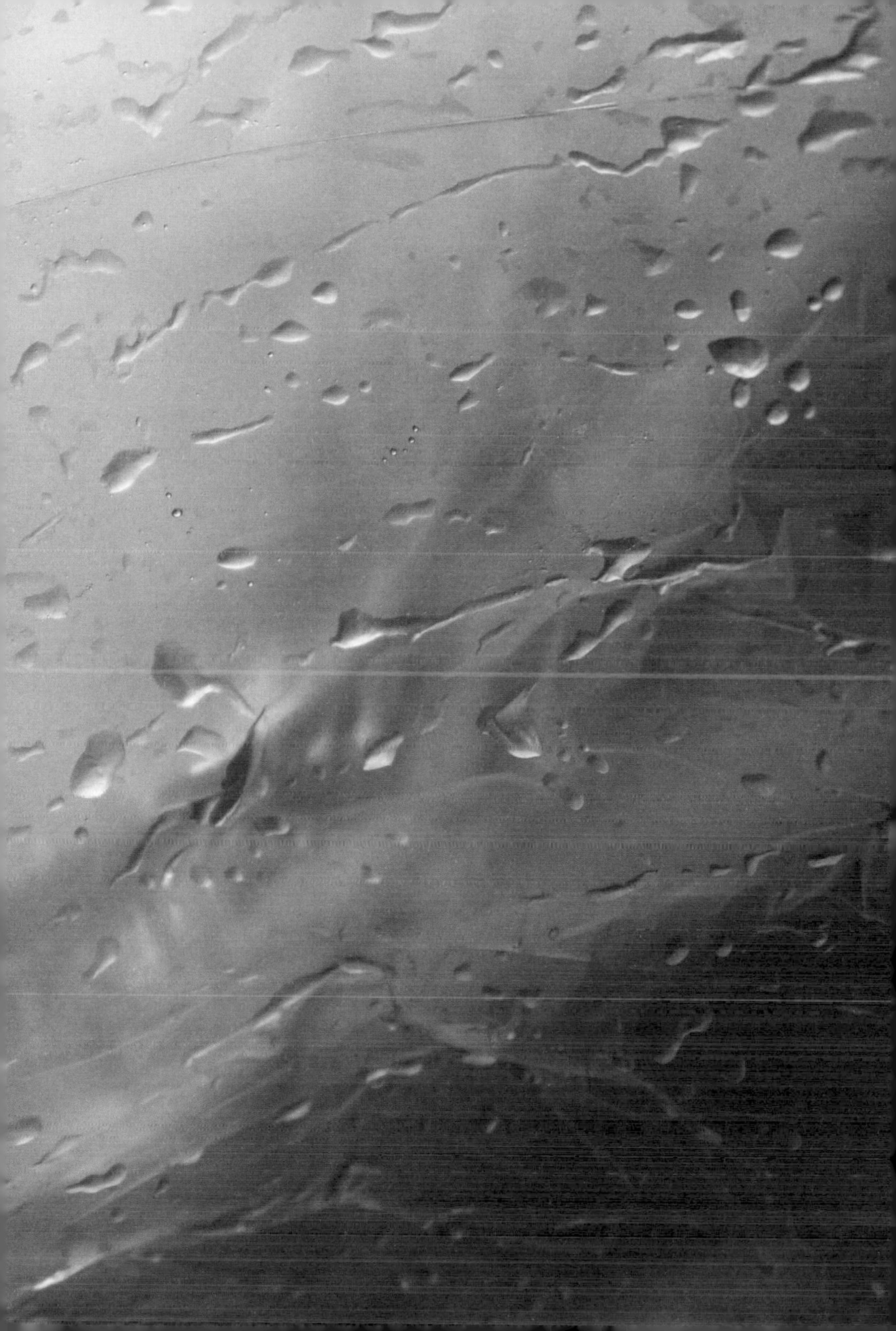

- You may start to find a new appreciation and wonder for water, discovering experientially rather than conceptually that all forms of water are part of a chain of natural and manmade conditions. Clouds are necessary for an ice cube to clink against the glass in your evening drink. You might like to reflect on all the conditions and natural or manmade processes that had to occur to make that ice cube, for example …

- … or the tear in your eye. Your body is mostly water and needs water to live. It takes it in and sweats it out. Even the blood pumping around your body contains 92 percent good-old H_2O. You, too, are a product of that cloud just as much as the ice cube.

CREATE:
PHOTOGRAPHY

You Will Need:

THE BASICS:
A camera or
mobile phone.

- Water is wonderful to photograph because it's constantly changing and never looks the same. The splatter of raindrops, the ripple of a stream, the crashing of waves, the soft settling of snow—there's so much to explore with our cameras that it's hard to know where to start.

- When you're out and about, be mindful of when and where you encounter water: puddles on the road, rain splashing against the car window, steam issuing from a vent. Pay attention to these with all your senses and photograph them.

- Why not choose one natural form of water (i.e., snow, rain, a river, the sea) and one manmade form of water (i.e., ice cubes, water from the shower, a faucet, a swimming pool), or choose forms that seem to be opposites in some other way, such as ice and mist. Use *Stop Look Breathe* to find the interconnectedness between the two. Take time to reflect on the conditions and forces that shape each. How do they come to be here, in front of you, right now? Then, *Create* a photograph.

CREATE:
DRAWING

Read the exercise for more details about what tools and media you may want to use for this *Create* activity.

- As we practice *Stop Look Breathe* with water, we start to become aware of reflections, colors, and textures on its surface and in its depths: the sea mirrors back the blue sky; the lake, once still and flat, now ripples as the wind blows over it. Notice how the surface of water reacts to and reflects the world, how colors change, and new textures appear constantly.

- For this mindful drawing project, we'll be turning attention to these aspects and exploring new ways of mark-making, so here are some slightly more detailed instructions on art materials.

- Gather together some non-traditional implements for putting marks on paper. Paintbrushes and pens are banished for now. Try old rags and scraps of cardboard, sticks, toothbrushes, pipe cleaners, paperclips, feathers … the crazier the better!

- You're going to dip all of these into drawing ink or paint. If you choose paint, use water-based acrylics or gouache so you can mix washes of color. You'll need some yogurt containers, old plastic water bottles, or jam jars for mixing and pouring these. If they have screw lids, all the better. You'll be able to transport them more easily.

- It's better to work live rather than from photographs, so visit a swimming pool, pond, puddle, river, lake, or ocean near you. *Stop Look Breathe* with it for a long time before you make any marks. Pay special attention to the colors you see in its depths and on the surface. Notice the reflections and the textures of the water.

- Previously, we may have focused more on line and form, but this time we'll focus only on color, texture, and marks. It's rather as if we're being Impressionists, showing the essence of the water as it flows and changes, less concerned with shape or structure. In this spirit, lay mark on top of mark, color on top of color, so that your drawing, too, is in a constant process of change and flow. Don't worry if it looks messy. Just use the drawing process to mindfully see and understand the nature of water.

- Experiment with different ways of making marks. See what you can do with a toothbrush, for example: scrub it, flick it. Roll up your rag into a point, use it like a sponge, or lay it out flat and blot or draw through it with a stick. Try pouring your paint directly onto your paper, put a layer of ink on the page and then scoop some off, or make marks into it with your cardboard.

- You can also try drawing onto wet paper - just dampen it with a sponge. Ink and paint bleed and flow in exciting new ways on wet paper, allowing us to become more mindful of the fluid nature of the materials we're using.

- Stay mindful of each new way of mark-making. *Stop Look Breathe* with it. How does it feel in your body? Which do you enjoy the most? And which marks do you like most when they end up on the page?

- Be aware that you'll need to make marks rapidly, without analyzing. Just reach for your materials instinctively, releasing the idea of controlling it, and simply be. This is great for practicing letting go.

Watching the ripples and movement of the water in the pond and mark-making with liquid acrylic onto wet and then dry paper

CREATE:
WRITING

You Will Need:

THE BASICS:
A pen or pencil,
notepad or journal,
and some scissors.

- After several activities where we were free writing and getting in the flow, in this project we're going to see how free writing can turn into poetry. I've used this technique in hundreds of classes and it works even for people who've never written a poem in their life or think they haven't got a poetic bone in their body.

- The first thing to realize is that most modern poetry doesn't rhyme and doesn't have a particular meter (or rhythm). It's called free verse, and that's exactly the right kind of poetry for mindful writing.

- Secondly, we don't have to reach for flowery, poetic language. Simple everyday words are far more powerful. This means your poems will sound like your voice, and that's very important.

- Thirdly, you don't have to come up with concepts. Just as before, you can write from the senses and from personal experience.

- Go sit with water and *Stop Look Breathe* with it, paying mindful attention with all your senses. Then, free write about it for 10–15 minutes. Memories of water may come into your writing, or ideas and images. It may even just be a straight sensory description. Any of these are perfect for this activity.

- Once you feel complete with your writing, read back over what you've just written and mindfully notice if any inner criticism comes up, and take time to *Stop Look Breathe* if it does. When we free write, we don't read back while we're writing, but now we're in the drafting stage so it's okay.

smooth sunned spots,
e surges, the heave,
the
silence far from sea*
n, the cutting line of
er bellies show
ancestral paths track
ction adust on the
shed by the sun.

ai
of
sea
wa
n w
taste
of
t w
r w
f
far

distinguishable
t ? just the
roil of condition
ow, current
wave, the next
to the tires. Silk, Bloate

ne – th
seen #,
counting
strike c

- Back at home, underline any parts of your free writing that you particularly like—phrases, whole sentences, even single words if one's really juicy.

- Now copy these fragments out onto strips of paper. Break your sentences up, making them into shorter lines. Try ending these new shorter lines with interesting words; choose "glisten," for example, instead of "and."

- Once you have all your strips, lay them out on a table and arrange and rearrange them into a sequence you like. Because your initial free writing was about a single subject, they should have coherence and fit together.

- Discard any that don't quite fit, or which repeat an idea or seem unnecessary. Keep moving bits of paper around until you're satisfied.

- You have now written a poem! You could even type this up, creating verses and redrafting it some more. Use strips of paper for the first draft though. It's more fun.

Here's the first draft of my poem on my kitchen table

tide shift undertow current

wave
line after line wave a diminishing perspective

etched on the backs of fishes . If I laid

a sheet on the dips & ridges

on the surface heave like zinc

cresting breaching all salt shiver

Plankton a dust

on the metal surface, on the sunned spots,

the surges, the cutting line of fin,

Would their silver bellies show — collodial

burnished. And if

you'd never seen it Would you ~~extrapolate~~
imagine

from ~~the~~ warm bath soak, from the brown
your

wood trickle of a stream, from —

your own tears, the suck

of a baby's mouth — or a lovers'

this
   silky bloated gritty stinging bright
 ^

never heard never tasted

PRACTICING MINDFULNESS:
Flowing with Our Emotions

Remember how I suggested that water related to our emotions? Let's return to that image again. When we're in a mindful state of awareness, simply being, our minds are like an expanse of clear water and our emotions are the colors that reflect in it. A swirl of red anger, a whirlpool of gray fear, a placid green expanse of joy—our emotions flow through us and our mindful awareness is the clear water that somehow holds and relects what's in the depths.

Our awareness is not the anger. It is not the fear. It isn't even the joy. We are simply aware of all these feelings. We need to stay emotionally alive not cut ourselves off from feeling, but even as we feel, we can learn to see emotions as reflections in a pond, or like the energetic rush of white water in a river—sometimes beautiful, sometimes frightening, but always just flowing through, passing by. During this project, take time to do the following and see how it changes your relationship to your emotions:

- *Stop Look Breathe* with the water, noticing how colors are just reflections and how they shift with light and weather, how textures change depending on the winds and currents. None of these aspects are actually the water itself; the water simply holds them.

- *Stop Look Breathe* with yourself and notice what your inner weather is like. What mood or emotion is there? Take time to *Breathe* with this, allowing yourself to see your emotions and your thoughts as the results of inner weather or atmospheric conditions rippling across the water of your awareness.

- Can you turn your attention to your awareness itself? Can you catch yourself being aware of your emotions, even fleetingly? With practice, this will become easier and you'll be able to stay connected to that aware part of yourself for longer.

- Notice that when you're aware, the emotions are still there. You can still feel them, but they become color, reflection, and texture in your awareness. Be the gentle, clear water holding the stormy sky of a stressful day. Be the bright clear water holding the reflection of a happy time with a close friend.

- Remember that being mindful doesn't mean disconnecting or withdrawing from our emotional lives; it just puts them into perspective.

- Through your week, whenever you become aware of your emotions, see if you can spend a few moments seeing them in this way and connecting with the clear water of your awareness, the stillness and clarity of simply being.

Final drafts (like this one) can often seem far removed from the original freewriting but still retain their vivid sensory qualities thanks to their roots in mindful observation.

Impression

If I laid paper on it
tide-shift undertow current
on etched dips and ridges
a surface heave like zinc
salt a shiver of dust
on metal would it show
colloidal silver burnished?

And if still
you hadn't seen it could you
imagine from a steaming
bath soak your own tears or
the suck of a lover's mouth—this cold
silky bloated gritty stinging bright
never heard never tasted.

PROJECT 6

The light of our lives

In this project, we'll be bringing our mindful attention to light, the fire of life. From the sun and bonfires, to lightbulbs and candles, we'll explore light and the warmth it creates in our lives. After learning to focus on the flow of emotions in the previous project, we'll be turning our attention to feelings once again, this time learning how to keep connecting with positive emotions so they have a chance to grow and warm our life too.

STOP—LOOK—BREATHE

- Bouncing off windows, dancing among the shadows at our feet, warming our bodies, light is the point where the fire of the sun meets the fire of our lives. Bring your mindful attention to light and begin to notice how it affects your mood, mind, body, and emotions. Check in with yourself on bright sunny days and on cloudy overcast days. How do they each affect you?

- Become aware of the light through your eyelids before you open your eyes and start the day, taking a little time to *Stop Look Breathe* and savor the sensations of waking.

- Turn your attention to transparency and refractions— how the light bounces off or passes through things, making them glow dully or even shine. Begin to notice the chinks and cracks where the light gets in (as Leonard Cohen said, there's one of those in everything).

- We often talk about a person being the "light of our life," but rather than *who*, ask yourself *what* is the light of your life? What makes you happy? What makes you glow? Perhaps it's the sound of a blackbird, spring trees, or the smell of rain (some of my personal favorites). Pay as much attention to the little things, as the big things. In fact, pay more attention to the little things. Let them become the small but regular pleasures that fill your days. Spend some quality time with these things that make life good and *Stop Look Breathe* with them so they have the maximum effect.

CREATE: PHOTOGRAPHY

You Will Need:

THE BASICS:
A camera or mobile phone.

- Firstly, photograph light in as many different forms as you can think of or find. You could capture window squares of sunlight on the floor, sunshine glinting in the fresh drops of rain in the grass, or shine a flashlight through things and explore translucency—anything from leaves to your own hand—or fill glasses with water and notice how the light refracts and distorts as it passes through. The possibilities are endless, so *Stop Look Breathe* with them, noticing the effects of light on your body, mind, and emotions as you enjoy its appearance and visual effects.

- Next, make a list of the things that are the light of your life, whether it's flowers, cats, or the ocean, and then seek them out and photograph them.

- When we're mindful and open to the world, we receive more of it—more beauty, more peace, more luminosity—so you may find new things to light up your life as you go about this activity, suddenly discovering that you love soft green moss, or that the neighbor's dog runs with such wonderful, lolloping joyfulness that you can't help but smile. Add these things to your list and photograph them if you can. This list and its accompanying images can be your feel-good storehouse for days you're feeling down.

- If some of your favorite light-up-your-life things aren't things you can see—like my favorite blackbird song—add them to your list anyway and make time to *Stop Look Breathe* with them too. If you think of an image that will capture that essence and remind you of that thing, go ahead and take it!

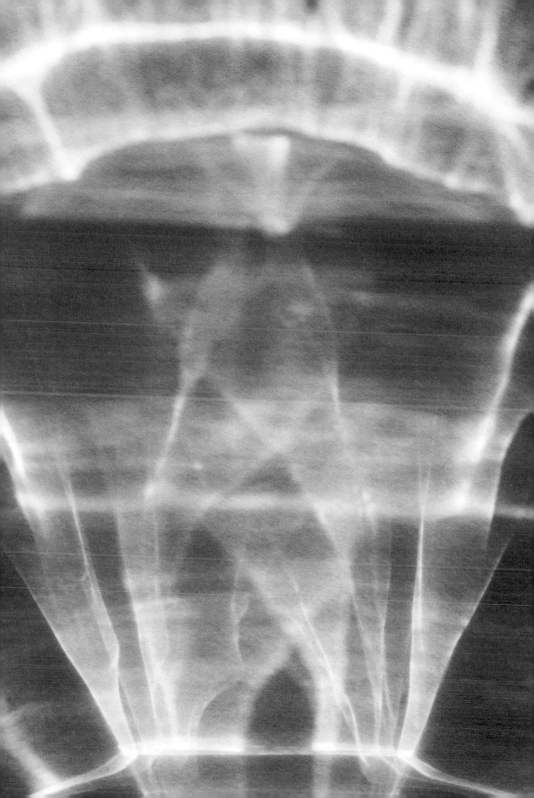

CREATE: DRAWING

You Will Need:

THE BASICS:
A sketchpad and the drawing media of your choice (i.e., pencil, charcoal, pastel, crayon).

For this *Create* activity, gather up a selection of some of the drawing tools we have used elsewhere in the book that you most enjoyed. And, of course, bring a sketchpad or other paper to draw on.

• So far, we've been paying attention to things that clearly and obviously light up our lives, and you may also have noticed that countless small pleasures and subtle beauties start to come to your attention as you become more mindful. Please do go and draw them. As you do, remember that this mindful drawing isn't about making a perfect reproduction but about spending time building a relationship with what you draw. Let your drawing bring you closer to your favorite things. Let it help you understand and cherish them even more. What ends up on the paper is of less concern that this warm opening to the world.

- And now I'm going to set you a little challenge: Find the light and beauty in things you might not normally. As we go about our lives, we overlook many things, dismissing them as routine, ordinary, boring, or even ugly. Your second mindful drawing activity for this project is to engage with the things you'd usually dismiss and see what you find there.

- Take yourself out for a *Stop Look Breathe* walk and keep an eye out for something you find ugly or unpleasing to the eye. Maybe it's a refuse sack torn and gutted, its contents all over the street; or a dingy wall, the brickwork stained with years of grime; or perhaps there's hideous wallpaper in the house you just bought but you can't afford to paint yet.

- Draw the thing you find ugly using a combination of the drawing techniques we've used so far. For example, you could combine drawing just color and texture with your rags and then over this, in another layer, draw just line and form with charcoal without looking at the page.

- Spend real time with your "ugly" thing, looking at it closely and mindfully in a way you wouldn't normally. See how you feel about this thing when you've finished drawing it. You might not suddenly be in ecstasy over the greasy pizza boxes littering your street or the wallpaper on your walls, but I suspect your relationship to the thing you chose will have changed subtly, that you will have noticed something about it that you wouldn't normally have, maybe even something surprising or possibly even lovely.

- You can try the same activity with something boring, something so ordinary that you wouldn't normally stop to look at it. Again, see how mindfulness changes your relationship to it.

Drawing with ink and fingers turned black mold on a wall into intricate blooming circles

- When we reach beyond ourselves in this way, mindfully and deliberately seeking the light in even the most unlikely of places, we inevitably find it ... maybe not all the time, but often. That is the secret joy of *Stop Look Breathe Create*; nothing is ordinary, nothing is beneath our notice. There's a crack in everything, but that's how the light gets in. We just have to look for the crack.

CREATE: WRITING

You Will Need:

THE BASICS:
Post-it notes and
something to
write with.
EXTRAS:
Luggage tags, scrap
paper, a hole puncher,
and string.

- What follows is one of my favorite mindful writing exercises: "Post-it Haiku." Haiku is an ancient, short form of poetry from Japan. Though seemingly very simple, they originally had a very strict form: seventeen syllables in three lines of five, seven, and five syllables, traditionally evoking images of the natural world. However, the art of haiku writing has spread and evolved over hundreds of years, and now many western contemporary poets use this form.

- With Post-it Haiku, we don't have to worry about the number of syllables, we just focus on being mindful of sights, smells, sounds, touch, and taste and then we free write three short lines about our observations that will fit on the paper.

- Post-it Haiku don't just have to be about the natural world, either. They can be about anything. For this project, let's continue o focus on light and on the small but simple things that give us that warm feeling of positivity in our chest.

- This is a particularly lovely exercise to do in your own home, workplace, or at a friend's house. Wander around, *Stop Look Breathe*, write your three short lines, and then (the important bit) stick your Post-it Haiku next to the thing you've just written about. Leave your Post-its for others to find, or for you to read and reconnect with through your day. Many of my students make one Post-it Haiku a day their daily mindfulness practice.

- In workshops, we often do this outside, using paper luggage tags instead of Post-its, and tying them to the things we love. When we leave, we leave the haikus fluttering in the wind on rose bushes, park benches, railings, and more.

PRACTICING MINDFULNESS:
Developing Positive Emotions

Mindfulness naturally helps us to develop more emotional positivity and resilience. When we have an experience that feels positive—emotions of joy, peacefulness, warmth, relaxation, and wellbeing—we can enhance these even more by bringing a greater mindfulness to them. By holding them in our awareness even for just a minute, we begin to rewire our brains, making positive emotions more possible in future.

The activities in this project are designed to connect you with your sources of light and positivity. To enhance this, when you feel a sense of satisfaction, enjoyment, inspiration, expansion, enthusiasm, happiness, peace, or any other positive feeling you encounter while creating, take time to *Stop Look Breathe* with it. This positivity may be anything from a feeling of a little more relaxation and softness in certain parts of the body to outright joyfulness.

- **STOP** and notice where you feel this positivity in your body.

- **LOOK:** Bring your attention to this sensation and notice what it's really like. Where does happiness occur for you? In your stomach? Your chest? The tips of your toes? What does enthusiasm feel like? Light? Fizzing? Buoyant?

- **BREATHE:** Rest your mindful awareness in these positive feelings in the body and really feel them by breathing and expanding into these areas on an in breath; then breathe out from these areas on an out breath. Stay with the feelings for about a minute or until they dissipate. Then continue with your creating.

- You can also do this with positive experiences at any time in your day, not just while creating. Perhaps you're happy to run into an old friend; *Stop Look Breathe* and savor it for a minute.

  Maybe you got some great feedback from a colleague at work; *Stop Look Breathe* and enjoy that feeling of pride and satisfaction.

- The more we pay attention to these feelings of positivity and the more we focus on the light in our lives, the more we change the way our brain works and the happier and more resilient we become.

PROJECT 7

In the shadows

We can't have light without shadow, and in this
project we'll be exploring how shadows and negative
spaces give shape to our world, to our photographs
and drawings, adding an extra richness to our
experience. We'll also turn our awareness to the
shadow sides of ourselves, learning to handle more
skillfully and kindly the shadows of negative
self-talk and feelings of being blocked that are
a common part of our creative lives, shining
the light of mindfulness on them all.

STOP—LOOK—BREATHE

- Start by becoming more aware of the shadow of each thing you encounter—cars, houses, cats, or trees—and take time to *Stop Look Breathe* with these shadows.

- Notice how on gray, overcast days the world loses its crispness as shadows become more diffused. I often feel as if the world around me has lost one of its essential dimensions on days like these, almost as if I was living in two dimensions instead of three.

- Become aware of your own shadow as it lopes at your feet throughout your day. Notice how it shrinks and lengthens, how it takes on the shape of your body and your movement. Our shadows are like mirrors that can help us become more aware of our bodies as they move through the world.

- Try some shadow yoga! Stand somewhere where you cast a shadow and make some slow mindful movement. Raise your arms and lower them, feeling how your body moves but also watching the corresponding movement in your shadow. Stretch and rotate. You could even do Tai Chi or dance. Whatever you do, keep your awareness both with the feeling of the body moving and the movement of your shadow.

- Throughout your day, keep a mindful eye on the shadows that move within you too, the shifting patterns of negative moods and emotions, of anxious or depressed feelings, the darkness of worry, self-doubt, or inner-criticism. Be kind to them.

CREATE:
PHOTOGRAPHY

- In this project, we're going to be exploring black-and-white photography. Working in monochrome helps us become more mindful of the range of tones—from black to white, from deepest shadow to most brilliant light—that the world possesses.

- So change your camera setting to black and white and take time as you do so to notice the difference between the color world you see through your eyes and the monochrome one you see through the screen. *Stop Look Breathe* and appreciate both.

- Make shadows your focus; you could choose one type (tree shadows, for example) or just photograph any interestingly shaped shadows that you encounter. I find that I often notice the shapes of things more when I photograph shadows. The curved necks and heads of streetlamps become strangely transformed and beautiful, while the shifting shadows under trees seem somehow more filled with movement and the chirp of birdsong than the leaves above my head do.

- You could also try creating a series of shadow selfies (using the approach outlined in Project 1—see page 38). Photograph your shadow on different surfaces and in different places.

You Will Need:

THE BASICS:
A sketchpad
and the drawing
media of your
choice (i.e.,
pencil, charcoal,
pastel, crayon).

CREATE:
DRAWING

Try any of the following drawing instruments for this *Create* activity:
an HB pencil, graphite, or charcoal and colored pencils, chalks, or
pastels. By varying pressure, you can get lots of tones from an HB
pencil or a single stick of graphite, but you could also try pencils or
graphite varying between hard and very soft.

- For this activity, we're going to explore shadows and negative
  spaces. Negative spaces are the spaces between or around things.
  If I put my hand on my hip, elbow out, then the negative space
  is the roughly triangular gap between the inside of my arm and
  my side. If I do this standing next to a wall, then there is another
  negative space between my whole body and the wall I am standing
  next to.

- Paying attention to negative spaces makes drawing easier since
  we can observe not only the shape of something but also the
  shape around it, making it more likely that our drawings will
  reflect what's actually there. Although creating a perfect copy
  isn't one of the primary aims of mindful drawing, seeing things
  clearly and with awareness is. Paying attention to negative spaces
  will help us do that.

- If you were to *Stop Look Breathe* with both the shape of my body and the negative spaces around it, you would be able to draw my outline in space, but without shadow, without shading, your drawing would still appear rather flat and two-dimensional. So, next you'd need to look at the light and shadow falling across me and fill these in, in order to give your drawing the appearance of three dimensions.

- If you find it difficult to see shadows or judge their depth (don't worry it takes practice!), then it might be helpful to make yourself a color (or rather shadow) chart. Draw a long, thin rectangle and divide it into five squares. Leave the first square white, make the last the darkest gray or black you can with your pencil, and make the three in between progressive shades of gray between white and black. You can use this to measure the shadows on the things you're drawing. (It can help to squint your eyes a little when you do this.) Leave the lightest parts of what you're drawing white, and make the darkest shadows black, and then shade in the other tonal areas in the mid-gray colors. This is a simplification of the numerous tones we find in life, but it can be very helpful to start with.

At school they made us draw tonal areas incredibly precisely with a standard pencil and I hated it. So for this little experimental sketch of plums I chose a thick, black, messy water-soluble crayon, working quickly, smudging with my fingers, finding the tones and shadows on the purple and golden skins, and enjoying myself enormously!

- Now that you know what you're looking out for, find some interesting objects to draw. I suggest you make some of them plain, smooth, curved objects as these are great for beginning to attune the eye to the gradations of shadow from light to dark. Then find some things that have intricate shapes with lots of negative spaces (the insides of seedpods or seashells can be great for this).

- Begin by working in monochrome, using charcoal, pencil, or graphite. As you draw, pay attention to the negative spaces around things. Move between these and the positive shape and solidity of the form they surround. Once you feel you've really seen and drawn these, then try adding shade to your drawing. Notice how filling in the shadows suddenly gives your drawing a more three-dimensional feel.

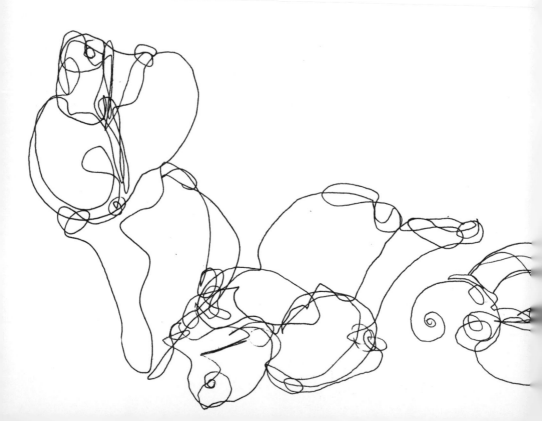

- When we draw light-colored objects, the changes in the tonal areas appear more distinct. On darker and colored objects, it can be a little more difficult. When we draw colored things, we start to notice that the shadows on them take on the colors of the object too.

- Finally, switch to your colored pencils or pastels and explore the different shades and tones you need to draw the shadows on the blue vase sitting on your windowsill, or even the face of your friend.

I used blind contour drawing to draw one shell over and over again, focusing on the negative spaces. As I did so the negative spaces revealed the spiral structure of the shell to me in a way I hadn't really noticed before.

CREATE:
WRITING

You Will Need:

THE BASICS:
A journal or
notepad and
something to
write with.

- Our familiar world seems so different at night, almost like another land. Without the hustle and noise of the daytime, sounds become intensified and it's hard to know where they're coming from or what's making them. Smells, too, are more vivid, with many plants only giving out their perfume once the sun has set. And with our dominant visual sense no longer quite as effective, our bodies become more alert, more mindful and sensitized. Yes indeed, there is another world to explore entirely in the shadows, so for this writing activity I'm inviting you to go on a nighttime *Stop Look Breathe Create* walk.

- When you do this, please make sure it's somewhere you feel safe. Why not take a friend with you and enjoy this activity together? Or if you have a backyard or garden, or you can borrow one, use this. Best of all for me is the countryside at night. Far away from people, traffic noise, and even the streetlights of the city, I can relax into a deeper darkness.

- Free write about this nighttime world. Tune in with all your senses, taking time to touch things, smell things, and listen intently. Try to rely on your visual sense least of all. As you do all of this, check in mindfully with your senses within the body, noticing how it feels to be out in the dark with no set purpose other than to experience the night.

Night writing in the dark, light out and suddenly my body feels longer, the inner dark and the outer dark merge, skin feels viscous and saturated, no longer a border, more a membrane something in me - no longer seen or visible - relaxes. Sounds come closer - traffic, cars, buses break apart into constituents, a whirr, rattle, a hum, a vibration - sound the darkness comes through the body, not just the ears, the space around me starts to become indeterminate - are things far away or close to me? Eyes shut everything is in close proximity intimate, the people - breathing entities, silent presences, a conspiracy of silence, of waiting, they seem closer here in the darkness than they do in the light, less separate. Yes, the darkness is a friend

COMING OUT
INTO THE HEAT
OF THE
ROAD
THE ROAD
THE SUN IS
RADIATING
OFF THE ASHPHALT
BAKING THE
SOLES OF MY
FEET. TRAFFIC
LOUD AND
INSISTENT.
MY HAT A HALO
OF BRIMMING
SHADE, EACH
PINPRICK
HOLE A

MINIATURE
SUN.

• We can also add a fun visual element to our daytime or night-time writing about shadows. Write a word at the top of your page, such as "streetlamp." This is what you're going to write about. *Stop Look Breathe* and draw the outline of the streetlamp's shadow beneath the word so it fills up the whole of the rest of the page. Now free write about the streetlamp and its shadow within the outlines of the drawing on the page so that you end up with a shape poem. I love doing these, and you can build up a succession of shadow writings on one page, overlapping your words, just as shadows overlap in real life.

I used some diluted ink to draw these shadows and then wrote over them in gray pencil.

LAMPPOST-A TILTING · · · · · · UFO LANDING IN THE LAST OF THE DAY'S SUNSHINE OR A ICICLE SINGLE EYE ON ME

PRACTICING MINDFULNESS:
Turning Toward the Shadows

Most of the shadows in our creative lives are ones we cast ourselves. We've already looked a little at our tendencies to judge and criticize our creative efforts, to doubt our abilities, strive too hard for perfection, and to hold on too tight. To these we might add avoidance, resistance, procrastination, fear of making mistakes, and even a sense of not being entitled to creative time—a sly, guilty voice that says, "You should really be helping the kids with their homework, studying, working, anything other than this self-indulgent creative mindfulness nonsense!"

Hopefully, you've found that finding a spacious, mindful breathing space (see Project 2 on page 50) has helped you deal with some of these internal negativities. Moving into the body and resting with the breath is always more helpful than going around in mental circles with these inner voices, but sometimes the cycle gets so powerful and goes on for so long that we just end up feeling we are totally and depressingly blocked. This feeling of being blocked is one that everyone experiences at some time in their creative life. Feeling blocked happens when a combination of circumstances, thought patterns, and emotions come together and build up until we feel we can't

I find pine cones a challenge to draw, but here I used my thick black crayon again and, squinting slightly to blur my vision, drew the shadow areas in the negative spaces, which gave me a much better sense of the mass and density of this lovely thing.

sit and meditate, can't draw or take a photo, and the thought of writing anything makes us want to run away.

How can we mindfully handle this most dreaded of the creative shadows? First off, we can begin by lightening up about it, gently and kindly acknowledging that there may be good reasons why we are feeling blocked. Bereavements, relationship troubles, and major life changes such as becoming a parent, changing jobs, moving house, and illness, to name a few, can and do impact our capacity to feel and act creatively.

Sometimes the reasons come from our past, from being too busy, not knowing how to get going again, or we may not know the reason why. However feeling blocked isn't something abnormal, so we can treat it as just another part of our creative life, seeing that the flow of our creativity varies depending on our life circumstances, energy level, and state of wellbeing. This can make this aspect of our personal shadows less frightening and less overwhelming.

Next, we can bring all the mindfulness, self-compassion, and emotional positivity we've been nurturing and turn toward the blocked feeling in a kindly way. I've found this act of turning toward an internal shadow to be very helpful at various times in my life. We have a very natural tendency to turn our back on the shadows, but when we turn toward them with all the caring and courageous mindfulness we can muster, the frightened parts of ourselves feel soothed, the hurts feel more tended to, and we mentally switch into an approach rather than avoid mode, which is a more creative and flexible state of mind.

Here's how to use *Stop Look Breathe* if your inner negative voices are seriously getting in the way of you enjoying your creativity, or if you feel you just can't create or meditate. You can do this if a blocked feeling comes up in the middle of drawing or writing a poem too.

1. **STOP:** Pause what you're doing. You can even walk away for a while and come back later. Do what's kindest and don't force anything. To this stopping you can also add the following mindful movements. Either cross your arms over your chest and gently rub the palms of your hands up and down your upper arms or place one palm on your solar plexus and one on the center of the chest. See which you find the most soothing. You can continue with these movements for the *Look* and *Breathe* parts of the practice too if you wish.

2. **LOOK:** With a kindly attitude, turn toward the blocked feeling, noticing the thoughts and emotions that are present without trying to change them.

3. **BREATHE** with these thoughts and emotions for just a few moments, feeling the spaciousness of the in breath. Dwell in your mindful awareness and notice any particular words, memories, or storylines that arise. They are just colors and textures in the water of mindfulness, remember? These thoughts or memories may be something you want to look at and reflect on later, but for now leave them be.

4. **LOOK AGAIN**, leaving the stories behind and shifting your focus to the physical sensations associated with them and where they are located in your body. For example, when I was life drawing at college, I used to feel a tense, hot feeling in my chest when I was being extremely critical of myself. If you can't clarify what you're feeling to that extent, then just notice if you feel a tense, contracted, or unpleasant feeling anywhere, particularly in your feeling space (the center of your chest and/or your solar plexus; see my explanation on page 69).

5. **BREATHE AGAIN**, connecting with the breath and, with as much warmth and understanding as you possibly can, turning toward the feeling in your body and surrounding it with the spaciousness of the in breath. This is a good point to bring in those mindful movements again if you aren't still doing them (from Step 1).

6. **THIS PLACE** you're turning toward is one of the most tender and vulnerable parts of yourself so be very, very gentle and see if you can let this blocked feeling in the body simply be another of the colors and textures in the water of your self-compassionate awareness.

7. **AS MUCH AS YOU CAN**, relax into the wide open space of the breath.

8. **DO** all of this only for as long as you feel you can stay with it. It may be just a couple of minutes. Then turn your attention toward the light, perhaps revisiting your photos and list of "light of my life" things or taking a walk somewhere peaceful and beautiful.

See what this mindful, self-compassionate "turning toward" meditation does for you. I make no claims that the feeling of being blocked will suddenly and permanently go; our minds and hearts aren't like a blocked drain that can be magically cleared after one go with a plunger and bleach. However, if we're patient, if we're kind, if we stop putting pressure on ourselves and simply pay attention to the little glimmers of light—the sudden impulse to write just a couple of lines, a desire to make space for a walk in nature, to do something playful with a friend, or take some photos of a sunset—then over time, the blocked feeling usually clears. Nothing lasts forever and the whole of life is in a constant flow of creative change. You are no exception.

PROJECT 8

The beauty of the broken

All of life is in a process of creative change and Stop Look Breathe Create helps us become more aware of this. The seasons pass and winter gives way to spring, the plant on our windowsill dies, but outside on the apple trees there is the green swell of new fruit; a dull, lethargic mood in the morning gives way to a peaceful feeling by the afternoon. In this project, we'll be celebrating the transience of life by paying special attention to the beauty of the broken, treating it as a window into life's changeable nature.

STOP - LOOK - BREATHE

- *Stop Look Breathe* has probably already sensitized you to the small but subtle beauties of the world. For this project, begin to pay special attention to the things you see around you that are visibly in a process of change, decay, evolution, or metamorphosis. Also look out for things that are broken, rusting, flaking, moldering, and getting old.

- In the Japanese Zen tradition, these things have a special name; they are said to be *wabi-sabi* and are celebrated because, in them, the impermanent, imperfect and incomplete can be seen and felt deeply. Wabi-sabi has been the inspiration for poetry and visual art for centuries, and, in perhaps its most moving form, it gave rise to the art of Kintsugi, in which the cracks on old, broken ceramics are mended with pure gold so that what might have been considered a flaw, a reason to be discarded, is turned into a thing of beauty to be treasured and celebrated.

Scars are very wabi-sabi. This page shows a brick scar, just a raw gash on a supporting wall where there was once a house; and next page—a moss scar, the plant pushing up through old paintwork.

- My favorite wabi-sabi thing is an old gate near my apartment, which I've been enjoying for about seven years. Each year, I've seen how the paint fades and flakes into more and more beautiful fractals of color, how the hinges rust, shading from deep brown to bright orange. Just a few weeks ago, it finally collapsed, and its boards now lie broken and exposed like ribs. The process of change has continued as the wood rots and plants grow up through it. It becomes something else every day.

- In the Project 7 writing activity (see page 140), I suggested you combine a little drawing with your writing (sketching the outline of shadows before writing inside them). In this project and the ones that follow, I'm going to encourage you to experiment with combining your photography, drawing, and writing in a creative mix of media and materials. Wabi-sabi, which is all about the "thingness" of things—their materiality as they change in the world—is the perfect place to start experimenting with this way of creating.

- However, the core practice is still the *Stop Look Breathe Create* method of being with the world and with your body, breath, and sensory experience with complete attention. This always comes first, so if you prefer to keep things simple and just use one media, ignore the mixed-media tips that follow.

Sewing like this is another way of drawing. You could try taking a needle and thread out with you instead of a pen.

CREATE:
PHOTOGRAPHY

You Will Need:

THE BASICS:
A camera or
mobile phone.

- Find something that seems in a process of changing—rotting, rusting, peeling, breaking, coming apart, etc. *Stop Look Breathe* with it, taking in this evidence of the ever-changing nature of things in this world.

- How can you capture this fleetingness, this process of change with your camera? Maybe you could photograph this thing over a period of time? Or perhaps a particular camera angle or setting would best convey what you're seeing, such as using monochrome or even a digital filter.

- Mixed-Media Tips: Try printing your photographs out onto different types of paper. Which papers best capture the wabi-sabi textures? Brown paper? Old newspaper? Textured or handmade paper? Photocopy your printed photos. This will start a process of degrading your image, making it more pixelated. How far could you take this? How about soaking your images in water and letting the colors run? You could also tear, and collage your photos, further embodying the process of change, the textures and beauty of the broken. Whatever you do, try to keep your image manipulation as low-tech as possible, let it embody the spirit of wabi-sabi which is all about the changing material nature of things (not sitting for hours with Photoshop!).

The texture on the back of an old envelope brings out the textures of this rusted metal and old paint perfectly.

CREATE:
DRAWING

Choose the drawing tools and supplies that you feel best suit your subject.

- Return to the wabi-sabi subjects you photographed, revisiting them and coming into a closer relationship with them through the lengthier process of drawing. Or, you can choose some different things to draw.

- One of the delights of wabi-sabi things is the amazing texture that emerges as materials change. You may like to revisit some of the approaches to drawing you used in Project 4 (see page 90) and to again draw as you did in Project 5 (see page 106), seeing your drawings not as things to finish, but as processes of change on the page.

- You could also choose organic thing, such as a piece of fruit, drawing it at regular intervals over a period of days or (even better) weeks. Show in your drawings the changes it goes through over time.

Tree burls are caused by fungi or parasites, which distort the wood but create a beautiful grain. They're the ultimate tree wabi-sabi! I drew this tree over a text about how they're formed, highlighting key words with watercolor.

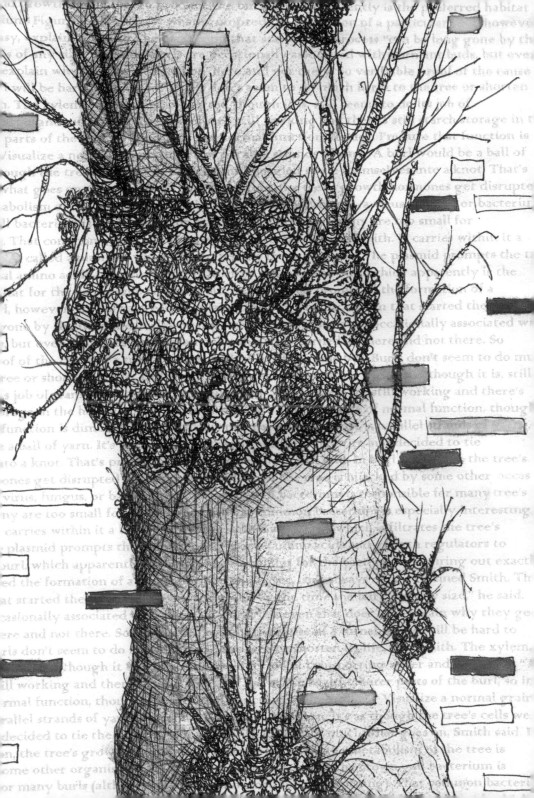

- Mixed-Media Tips: Why not try ripping or tearing your drawings and then joining them together again in a way that celebrates the tears, just as they do with Kintsugi ceramics? You could use gold paint mixed in with glue, or even (if your paper is thick enough) sew them together with embroidery thread. You could do the same for any "mistakes" you make when you're drawing. Instead of sighing and rubbing them out, treating them as a flaw, turn them into something beautiful, perhaps with an expressive imaginative doodle around it, a highlight in a contrasting color, or a single spot of brightly colored paint.

- More Mixed-Media Tips: You could also try drawing over the photocopied or collaged images you created for the photography activity in this project, adding your marks on top as a second layer, as I did here with this drawing of fungus. Try laying some white acrylic paint or artists' gesso as a thin basecoat over parts or all of your photographic images. This will mean your drawing stands out strongly in some places, fading into the background textures of the printed image in others.

I found a tree with a ring of fungus which I photographed and then drew using gesso, charcoal, and gel pen. The colored ink made beautiful the things I might have viewed as "mistakes," and changed how I saw my drawing.

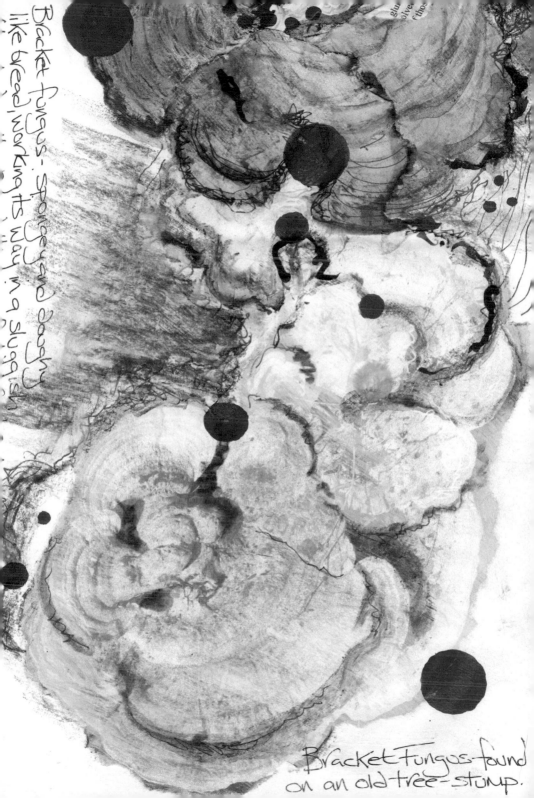

Bracket Fungus - Spongey and doughy like bread, working its way in a sluggish

Bracket Fungus - found on an old tree-stump.

CREATE:
WRITING

You Will Need:

THE BASICS:
A journal or
notepad and
something to
write with.

- *Stop Look Breathe* with something you see to be in a process
  of change, something that is, or is becoming, wabi-sabi.
  Free write a few lines about it and then pause. Look within.
  Reflect on the different ways that you are changing and
  becoming wabi-sabi. Free write a few lines about this.

- Alternate between writing about what you're looking at and
  writing about yourself. You may choose to reflect on some or
  all of these aspects of your own experience and how they
  are impermanent and constantly changing: your thoughts,
  your emotions, your body, your habits, your beliefs, your
  relationships, and so on.

- At a certain point while you're writing, you might, if you're lucky,
  start to lose track of whether you're writing about your wabi-sabi
  thing or yourself. If this happens, go with it. Let the two merge
  and blend, so that when you're writing (for example) about the

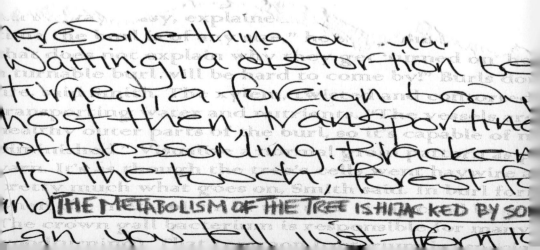

way the air eats away at the metal on the old bolt on your back door, oxidizing it, turning it to rust, you're also somehow writing about your feelings and how they're eroded by time, or circumstances, or even by mindfulness.

- When you've written for about 10–15 minutes, read back over your free writing and underline the bits you like the best, cutting and pasting and editing them on pieces of paper as you did in Project 5 (see page 110). You should find that a metaphor starts to emerge, that the poem you create about that old bolt on the door also speaks of a metaphysical process of change and transformation happening within you, or indeed, within all of us.

- Mixed-Media Tips: Why not photocopy your writing or try writing over your drawings and printed photos, then collaging them all together?

- More Mixed-Media Tips: In some countries, prayers are written onto long strings of brightly colored flags so they can be blown into the world on the winds. You could release your words back to the elements that created them by making poetry flags. Write the lines of your poem onto squares of scrap material (or copies of your drawings or photographs), one line for each square. Stick or sew your material onto string and hang your flags outside, where they'll be affected by the elements, until they become frayed and faded, wet and torn, a thing of poetic wabi-sabi beauty in themselves.

Next page: photocopies of photographs, torn up, splashed with water, scrunched, collaged, and written over.

bulg
nis pot
rough skin—bar
fingers, body braille
HER ORGANISM – A VIRUS FUNGUS OR BACTERIUM.

I am a process of breaking dou
of ending, each flaking cell

my frayed places
discarded, serrated and chipping
I'm sloughed off rubbing against
My feet are dust

all my torn edges
peeling in
the world-eroded

PRACTICING MINDFULNESS:
Embracing Change

How has it felt to contemplate the nature of transience and change during this project? What have you discovered about your relationship to it? Do you resist change or do you embrace it? Sometimes reflecting on the impermanence of things can be frightening because, in doing so, we come face to face with the fragility of our own bodies, relationships, and of life itself. This awareness often lies below the radar of our everyday consciousness, but it's there. If we can *Stop Look Breathe* with it, we often find feelings of respect, appreciation, and even tenderness arising for the fleeting, beautiful,gone-in-a-moment life we are living. Everything becomes suddenly very precious.

At other times, the impermanence of things can be an enormous relief. When we're in pain, when we're suffering, when we're feeling lost, hopeless, terrified, confused, unsure, or unloved, contemplating this evidence of the fleetingness of all things can be tremendously reassuring. "This too will pass," the world seems to be telling us over and over again.

This is the beauty of wabi-sabi. It makes us mindful of what we might have a tendency to resist or ignore, and it has the potential to sharpen our awareness and our gratitude for the beauty and transience of life. It celebrates all the things of the world, the great and the small, for their cracked and flawed imperfections. It shines a light on us. It paints us gold.

- If any of this strikes a chord with you, or if you found it helpful or surprising, then why not make looking for, appreciating, and contemplating wabi-sabi things a regular part of your life?

- Or, simply be intentionally mindful of the changing cycles of life in the world around you, and of the cycles of life within you. *Stop Look Breathe* with these, too.

- Finally, we can bring this wabi-sabi awareness to all our creating as we did in this project, celebrating the flaws, being mindful that every act of creation is imperfect and incomplete —and thank goodness for that!

Becoming closer

As our mindful connection to the world grows, our sense of curiosity and appreciation for life increases, and we start to find a different way of relating to things. However, Stop Look Breathe Create doesn't only help us become mindful of things; it's also an invitation to a new way of relating to people. In this project, we'll explore this by extending our mindfulness out to the human world and discovering how it helps increase our empathy and feelings of connection in even the busiest and most disconnected of environments.

STOP—LOOK—BREATHE

- Most of us no longer live on a street where everyone knows our name, and our communities and families have become more fragmented. We don't walk to work or to the store, greeting neighbors as we go. Instead, we get in cars or sit on public transport systems, our faces lit by the screens of our smartphones. It isn't hard to see why feelings of disconnection, isolation, and loneliness are on the rise.

- In small, mindful ways, though, we can reverse this trend toward separation and disconnection by paying mindful attention to the people around us. (I give more detailed suggestions for this in the Practicing Mindfulness section at the end of this project on page 184).

  - Take time to *Stop Look Breathe* with the human world and see what you notice. People watching can be one of the great pleasures of life and, as we'll discover in this project, when practiced with mindfulness it can substantially alter the way we relate to the anonymous human crowd around us.

CREATE:
PHOTOGRAPHY

You Will Need:

THE BASICS:
A camera or
mobile phone.

- Let's start with some street photography, which is best done somewhere you can people-watch unobserved. Markets, railway stations, or busy streets are great for this. It's important to be mindful and sensitive to people's privacy and personal space, so if I feel I'm making anyone uncomfortable, I always stop.

- *Stop Look Breathe*, and also be aware that people move quickly. You'll have to stay alert and be ready to snap. This makes it a little harder to incorporate mindfulness in a slow, measured way, but you can compensate by returning to *Stop Look Breathe* as soon as you've taken a few photos of someone. In this way, street photography becomes a rhythmic process of connecting within and then connecting to the people around us, moving inward and then outward, like the breath.

- You could also *Stop Look Breathe* with your camera in your lap or at waist level, just pointing your lens in the right direction and clicking without looking at the screen. The results of this technique can be quite random; heads get cropped off, and sometimes people are half out of the frame, but the photos feel full of spontaneity and movement and I've taken some of my favorite photos this way.

- If you're feeling brave, ask an approachable stranger if you can take their portrait. Tell them you're following some photography exercises in a book and would they mind if you took a photo of them? By offering a reason (the book, "I'm just learning"), you open up the possibility for a little conversation and an opportunity to connect in a natural way. Be prepared for refusals as well as acceptances to these requests.

- If you choose to ask people for portraits, be mindful of your feelings about this. *Stop Look Breathe* with any shyness, nervousness, or embarrassment. You could share this feeling in your initial conversation: "I feel a little nervous asking you, but could I take a photograph of you for my project?"

- Go with your own intuition on who's approachable and who isn't. If in doubt, don't. Only ask people you feel comfortable and safe with. You could warm up in a familiar environment, such as a family party or a friend's cookout, before hitting the streets.

- Whoever you choose, remember to *Stop Look Breathe* with each person. Allow yourself to be fully with them.

- Mixed-Media Tips: Experiment with color and black and white. Try combining your mindful photography with mindful writing, by writing over prints of your photos with a white gel pen or acrylic marker, creating layered portraits of words and images. If you chat to the person you photograph, you could write down what you remember of the conversation around their portrait.

Bird Market. Hong Kong.

January 3rd.

I met Gina taking down
decorations in the hallway of
my friends' building. She's lived
there for more than 40 years, and
puts these up each Christmas.
There was tinsel everywhere,
wafting on the stair rail whenever
a door opened or closed. Lots of
fire, energy, and tough humor in her.
She laughed and gossiped loudly
with me, her hoarse, smoker's voice
echoing down the stairs, telling
me how the neighborhood had
changed, old families moving out
and new rich people coming in as
it was gentrified. I asked, could I
take her photo? And if she thought
it a little odd, she also seemed
pleased and did so happily.

CREATE:
DRAWING

- This project is all about increasing our awareness and sense of connection to others, and since we're concerned with relationship rather than "accuracy," start by returning to the blind contour and continuous line drawing techniques we used earlier in this book. (You may never have left them.)

- To your list of locations, you might like to add cafés, libraries, trains, waiting rooms, bus stops—places where people aren't moving around as much, giving your pencil a chance to get to know them.

- I love sketching people. It's my absolute favorite drawing practice. And for those too shy for street photography, it's a more gentle way of becoming closer. See who catches your eye. Is it the bearded guy in glasses sipping his cappuccino, or the young mother with a sleepy toddler on her lap? Use some of the Practicing Mindfulness tips at the end of this project (see page 184) before you begin to draw.

- Give yourself two or three minutes for each sketch. *Stop Look Breathe* and draw without looking at the page and in a continuous line. Then in the next quick sketch, try looking at the page occasionally to orient your pen, then finally with about 50/50 looking and not looking. Use the continuous line as much or as little as you want.

- Allow your drawing process to reveal to you the proportions and gestures of the human body as it sits or stands. Draw what you see rather than trying to work out how it's all connected.

- Be prepared for people to move at inconvenient moments, or even to leave! You may not get as much as two or three minutes, so get used to drawing rapidly, instinctively, and without any expectation that this drawing is going to be finished. Just enjoy the time you spend with each person.

- How about drawing commuters waiting in line for a bus, or that cluster of teenagers hanging out with their skateboards? When drawing groups, don't try to draw everything, instead view them as a single body, drawing the main outlines of body shapes—heads, legs, the bulge of a backpack, the curve of an umbrella—and all the negative spaces in between. Then add in key details, like the silhouette of a face beneath a baseball cap here, a hand clutching a handbag there. If people move, don't worry; just keep looking and drawing.

- Mixed Media Tips: When you're on location, move between writing and sketching, allowing them to overlap on the page. You could use two contrasting colors for the writing and drawing. If after a while your page gets too busy in places, try blanking these areas out with white acrylic or artist's gesso, working over it again once it's dried. Long strips of paper stuck into your sketchbook can be great for this activity so that your crowd spills out of the pages and into the world.

Blind contour drawings of people can be weird as well as wonderful but always capture something of their character and body language.

Everyone poised & expectant, eyes on the departures board shifting from leg to leg

The trundle of suite
-the hollow echo of

Brighton Station

You Will Need:

THE BASICS:
A notepad or
journal and
pen or pencil.

CREATE:
WRITING

- *Stop Look Breathe* and free write about the people around you, how they move and gesture, the facial expressions they make, the clothes they're wearing, the emotions, moods, or personalities you deduce from your encounter with them. Use the Practicing Mindfulness suggestions at the end of this project to help you do this (see page 184).

- Pick one person, or two who are together, and take a little more time to *Stop Look Breathe* with them. Who are they? Here is the point where mindful writing based on the senses can enter the realm of the imagination as we ask ourselves a series of questions: *What* is the relationship between these two? Or *why* is this person here on their own? *Where* do they live? *Who* do they live with or do they live alone? If they seem to be in a good mood, *why* are they in a good mood? If they're looking depressed, again, *why*? Allow your imagination to supply spontaneous answers and write these down. Ask yourself more what, where, when, why, who, and how questions.

first, just seeing, being with. They seem solid these 2 sisters, twins, there's something so strong about the way they sit there, side by side. The way they're holding the newspaper! Two halves, two hands, two minds united in the act of reading. The complementing colors of their clothes, the same taste, different choices. **WHO?** There's a groove of deep familiarity about how they sit here. Perhaps they come every day, buy a paper, sit on bench under the wall of

Always together. close by per- apartment TURN THE PAGE — other ways HOTELS **WHAT?** the 'A troublesome — y were young dging, aggressive on the door talk it over. Or

- Use this question activity to create a portrait of a fictional character based on the person you've been focusing on. You could then imagine your character leaving the place you are sitting and heading out into the world. Who are they going to meet? What happens when they do?

- Keep your imaginative writing mindful by checking in with your body and breath from time to time, noticing how you're feeling and if any inner criticism is arising.

- In this way we can use our mindful writing and the sense of empathy and connection it creates as the launch pad for creating characters and stories. I wrote a little flash fiction based on the mole I saw on the arm of a man on a train. Whole novels can start from a chance encounter, from really seeing someone and connecting with them with awareness and openness.

GARY had a tattoo. A sleeve of BLUE shifting ink, a skinful of waves. In the MIDDLE marooned on a PATCH of freckled skin, a MOLE. A fleshy island - which when I first knew him - I TRAILED FINGERS towards. When I touched it the sea retreated LAPPED back, and GARY would gasp and grab MY HAND. Back then I had the power to TURN the TIDE. Now he wears long shirts that BUTTON at the WRISTS.

PRACTICING MINDFULNESS:
Connecting Mindfully with Others

Here's how to turn people watching into mindfulness practice:

- *Stop Look Breathe* with the movements and energy of many people in a space. See who catches your eye. Is it the old lady in the bright pink raincoat, pushing a shopping cart? Is it the teenage boy, hunched on the end of a bench and staring at his feet?

- What is it that's drawn you in? Their body language? What they're wearing? Or is there something familiar about them? Do they remind you of your mother, or your brother, or yourself? *Stop Look Breathe* with all of these things—their movements, their appearance, any expressions or gestures that give you clues to who they are, what they're feeling, and how they're unique.

- *Look* and allow yourself to really see them, and take time to connect with yourself too, with your breathing, feeling body. Feel your own humanness, your own uniqueness, vulnerability, tenderness, and humanity. Move between being with yourself in this open, accepting way and turning your attention outward to being with this stranger in all their uniqueness, vulnerability, and humanity.

- Look for things you share. You're both hunched against the cold as you wait for your train. You're both heading home somewhere at the end of the working day. Maybe you're both hungry or sleepy.

- You could also reflect on the universal shared experiences of being human. This person gets lonely and wants to be happy too. This person needs to feel loved and they get sick and tired just like you do. They're also naturally creative and need to express this in some way.

- Notice if you're not feeling open to this person for any reason. Perhaps you're feeling a little closed off after a hard day, or they remind you of someone you find difficult. Maybe they seem a little "other" to you, different from you and the people you know. *Stop Look Breathe* and notice where you feel this shutting off to them in your body. It can often be felt as a hardness, a closed or resistant feeling.

A local street party was a great opportunity for photographing friends and neighbors and becoming closer.

- It's always interesting to discover that we've shut ourselves off when we could be feeling connected. Be gentle and understanding with yourself if you discover this. Sit with your breath, your body, and the feeling of being closed, and notice if it shifts or changes in the course of kindly being with yourself and being with this other person.

- Don't try and force feelings of connection. Don't feel that you must look at the masses and feel overwhelming love for them all. We're simply cultivating openness, being sensitive to ourselves and to others, finding small areas of connection and a willingness to see our shared humanity, the ways we're the same.

- We can also try wishing this individual well. This isn't praying, though you can make it a prayer if you want to. It's more about generating a sense of generosity and positive well-wishing. You could try saying to yourself in your head as you stand waiting for your train something like, "May this person get home to their cozy apartment soon. May they have a warm welcome. May they feel peaceful and relaxed at the end of their day. May they be well and happy. May they feel some love in their life. May they find some time for creativity." Notice how this well-wishing makes you feel. Try offering the same good wishes to yourself too! How does that feel?

- If you enjoy this experience of mindfully connecting with a stranger, you could try doing this when you're with someone you know—a friend, work colleague, or family member—bringing this same mindful sense of really being present with someone to the interaction. Notice how you are remaining open, listening and connecting, and also be mindful of any times you switch off or close off.

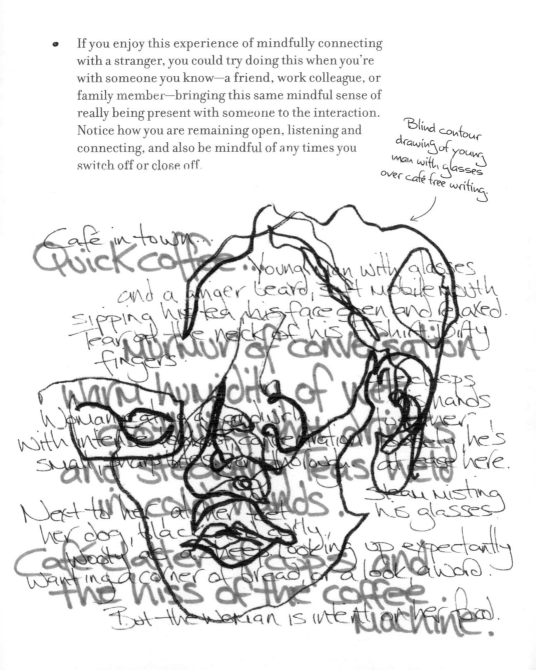

Blind contour drawing of young man with glasses over café free writing.

PROJECT 10

A sense of place

Here we are at our final project,
and in it you'll bring together everything
you've learned and experimented with so far
to explore a place with Stop Look Breathe Create.
This is a project that could be repeated
many times, with different locations providing
the inspiration you need to keep on creating
and being mindful well beyond the point
at which you've finished this book.

STOP—LOOK—BREATHE

- The possibilities for this project are limitless. What kind of place will you choose to explore? How about the block where you live, your local park, a national park or piece of wilderness, an overgrown empty lot, a local market, your university campus, the building you work in, the city you're visiting on vacation, or even your own home?

- Visit this place every day if you can for a period of time. Try to see it at different times of day and in all kinds of weather. If this is a one-off visit then it will be especially important for you to take time to simply be in it before you reach for your sketchpad, notebook, or camera.

- Use all the approaches we've explored in this book so far, encountering and spending mindful time with the many aspects of this place: the sky above, the ground below, and everything in between; the elements of air, water, earth, and fire; light and shadow; texture, color, pattern, and repetition. Encounter any people in this place mindfully and look out for signs of wabi-sabi—the old, broken, and impermanent—but also for new life, for the start of new cycles, and fresh things.

- *Stop Look Breathe* with everything you find and allow
  yourself to really be with this place, noticing its effect
  on you, on your body, mind, mood, and emotions, the
  ways you open to it, and the ways you close off, too.
  Find new ways of mindfully tuning into where you are
  and be as creative with this as you are with the *Create*
  parts of the practice: Try walking the perimeter, lying,
  sitting, and standing, listening for sounds, shouting,
  whispering, waiting for answers, touching things,
  leaning against them, looking at
  them upside down. Get to know
  this place inside out and let your
  photography, drawing, and writing
  help you with this.

I chose to make my project
book about the park I do my
Stop Look Breathe Create
walks in every day.

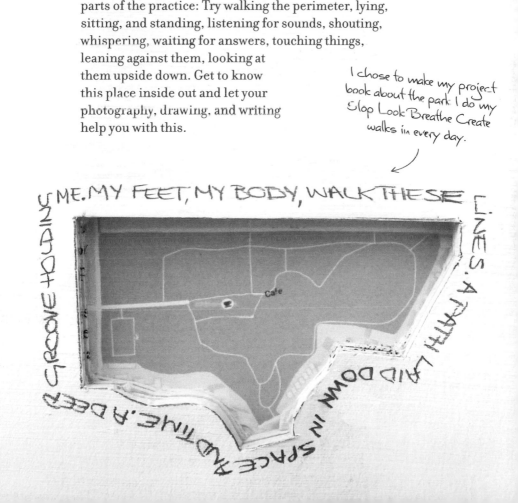

CREATE:

MIXED MEDIA IDEAS FOR A SENSE OF PLACE

Pull out all your creative tools for this *Create* activity and blend them freely.

- Why not make your own sketchbook or scrapbook especially for this project? You could even make it as you go along. Your project book could be large or small and for its pages you could use different types of paper, cloth, old newspapers and magazines prepared with white acrylic or artist's gesso, or even make your own paper.

- Keep your leaves loose or make a cover, binding them together any way you want: Put all the leaves in a box, staple them, sew them, punch holes through the tops and thread string through them so they hang like bunting, or keep adding pages to make a long concertina that keeps unfolding and unfolding. Be as imaginative and creative as you like with this; make it a *Stop Look Breathe Create* project in itself.

- By the end of the project, your book will carry the spirit of your chosen location so that if a stranger were to flick through its pages, they'd be able to get a sense of the place just from looking at it.

Small enough to fit in your hands—I made my little book in early Fall, and used recycled card, salvaged paper, and even leaves for pages to capture the colors and textures of the time of year.

A Sense of Place

COMBINING CREATIVE MEDIUMS

In the last two projects, we started to experiment with mixed-media approaches. In this project, you get to do it your way! If you prefer to keep your photos, drawings, and writing separate, divide your project book into three sections. Or, you might just want to do a single-media project and make it into a book. Create this project in whatever way you will most enjoy, and if you want to bring in media other than photography, drawing, and writing, please do. Whatever you've been longing to try, try it.

The previous projects should have given you some ideas about how you can start to combine media and make your "Sense of Place" project book. Here are some further suggestions as you continue:

- Layer words on top of images and images on top of words.

- Hand tint your black-and-white photographs with watercolor pencils or paint. Do this sitting back where you took the photo so the colors are true to life.

- Collage, montage, or make kaleidoscopic pictures from photo fragments.

- Try printing images onto different types of paper or onto acetate.

- Doodle, scribble, and let your hand be lead by your breath.

- Create textures and patterns inspired by what you see and then draw or write over them in contrasting colors.

I painted brown paper with white gesso and then printed my photograph on top. I used white pencil for my 6-word haiku.

→

each day
the leaves
piling up...

- Use thread instead of a pen to make lines.

- Draw outlines and silhouettes, then cut them out and stick them into other images.

- Stick found objects from your *Stop Look Breathe Create* walks into your book. Put them next to photos or drawings you've made of them.

- Play with materials: try tearing, wetting, perforating, sticking, or folding.

- Thread things through, hang things from corners, or make pockets and page extensions. Let your creativity escape the page entirely.

- Make holes for other pages to peep through.

- Who says pages have to be the same size anyway?

- Try some calligraphy and hand lettering, or cut out words from magazines that describe your place.

- Attach word fragments, poems, and haikus to the things you write about in your place, and then photograph them and put the photos next to these words or writings in your book.

- Free write and then circle the words and phrases you like, coloring them in with beautiful colors. Make poems by linking these with lines or numbers.

I collaged photos of leaf shadows and a real leaf, with scraps of material, my writing, and a drawing of a dogwalker, sewing them together on the page.

early Fall
morning
dog walkers
hold leashes
radial lines
criss-crossing
the grass

Whatever mediums you use, *Stop Look Breathe* with each one, noticing how it feels to use them, keeping in touch with your breath, pausing to enjoy the process, being mindful of how it feels to *Create* whether you're in your location or back at home. This project, like all the others in this book, is about process, not end results, so don't make your project book so precious that you can't "mess it up," explore and play. Save pages for wild leaps of imagination and weird creative experiments—rubbing textures, copying colors, doing free writes, taking a continuous line for a walk (even across several pages), doodling, splattering, sticking in lots of photos, collaging them and drawing and writing over them again. Project books and sketchbooks are about new ideas and new mediums. They are the places where we discover that mistakes and accidents are the innovations of creation.

Let your project book embody the process of *Stop Look Breathe Create*. This is what I've tried to do in this book as I illustrated it, choosing drawings, photos, and writing for you that shout about my process and experience of creating, rather than those that look like perfect illustrations. It can be challenging to create like this, to allow ourselves to be real and vulnerable on the page. So, as ever, when the feelings of insecurity and self-doubt come up, we practice *Stop Look Breathe* and become mindful of this, kindly soothing the parts of ourselves that need it.

At it's best, I have found that *Stop Look Breathe Create* opens the whole world to me and I become intimately and vibrantly alive to it. At it's best, *Stop Look Breathe Create* has lifted me out of creative doldrums and low moods. At its best, it has revealed to me the ways I remain disconnected from myself, my life, and my creativity, and it has offered me ways to reconnect. My life would be poorer without it.

And so, as this project draws to an end, I can only wish you everything that this simple but profound mindfulness practice has given me. May you find joy and freedom in your creating. May you find an ever-deeper mindful connection with yourself and with the world around you. And may *Stop Look Breathe Create*—these four easy steps—reveal the next creative adventure that's calling you.

PRACTICING MINDFULNESS:
Checking In and Moving On

How has taking part in these creative mindfulness projects affected you? If you've been doing a project a week, then you've been practicing now for two or three months. That's long enough for you to have formed some new mindful and creative habits, and to have given them a chance to establish themselves. Like small pebbles thrown into a pond, even little changes can ripple out to impact areas of our lives that might seem quite disconnected. Take some time to check in with yourself and reflect on your creative mindfulness journey during this time and how it's affected you. You might like to look back to the review you did at the end of Project 4 (see page 94) and compare now and then.

- What part of this practice has given you the most consistent pleasure? Can you make a plan to continue this weekly?

- What do you find most challenging? Has this shifted or changed at all since you originally asked yourself this question? Is the inner criticism easing off a little? Are you finding that making time to slow down and be kind to yourself with a little meditation in your day is happening more naturally?

- How has practicing mindfulness and self-compassion with your habitual patterns of thinking, feeling, or behaving around creating affected them?

- Has this habit of mindful, loving kindness spilled over into other areas of your life?

- Have you noticed any shifts in other seemingly disconnected areas of your life? Has this period of creativity and mindfulness changed how you work, exercise, or interact with others? Has your sense of general wellbeing improved at all? Do you get as stressed as usual, or have you found new strategies for coping with this?

- Conclude by choosing those mindfulness practices you feel are most beneficial and those creative activities you get most pleasure from and make yourself an action plan to keep you motivated and inspired.

- It might help to set *Stop Look Breathe Create* projects for four weeks at a time:

    WEEK 1: You might choose to go to your local park and draw, photograph, and write about trees.

    WEEK 2: This might be the week you've got a big deadline at work and are very busy, so you might feel that what you need is to sit with your morning tea and look out the window at the garden, simply engaging with *Stop Look Breathe* for five minutes then writing a single Post-it Haiku.

    WEEK 3: You might have a holiday planned—a perfect opportunity for lots of the *Breathe* part of the practice and loads of photography.

    WEEK 4: Just an average week, you might decide to print out some of your photos, collage them, and draw and write over them, spending some time with *Breathe* when you finish.

- Adapt and adjust your creative mindfulness to fit your life, and do remember that we have to make the time because time doesn't naturally make itself. Let the enjoyment, changes, and discoveries you've experienced through the projects in this book be the incentives to continue in future.

ACKNOWLEDGMENTS:

Firstly my deep gratitude and thanks to the mindfulness teachers, retreat centers and centers for practice that have guided my meditation and enriched my life over recent years, particularly Brighton Buddhist Centre. I have received so much, and hope I can pass on even a little of it.

Secondly, to my students, who turn up for themselves and their creativity with such courage and vulnerability, allowing it to be just as it is in the moment. I can only share what I've learned and you teach me so much.

Getting started thanks are due to Lela and Sandy for feedback on my first embryonic draft of Stop Look Breathe Create; and to Jake for connecting me up with the Ilex Team.

Love to my parents, sister, and nephews Jamie and William – I said I'd mention you in a book one day and here it is! Love to Ian. And love with a hand on my heart to Patrik, the only 6-toed one for me.

Finally my thanks to everyone at Ilex and Octopus: Zara for enthusiastically championing this book and helping me make my vision of it a reality; Hayley for editing so sensitively; Frank for keeping us on track, Mina for translating our ideas into a clear, peaceful, creative book space; and Lucy for seeing it through production. Deep bow to you all.